THE IMPORTANCE OF

Jane Goodall

These and other titles are included in The Importance
Of biography series:

Alexander the Great	Adolf Hitler
Muhammad Ali	Harry Houdini
Louis Armstrong	Thomas Jefferson
James Baldwin	Mother Jones
Clara Barton	Chief Joseph
Napoleon Bonaparte	Malcolm X
Julius Caesar	Margaret Mead
Rachel Carson	Michelangelo
Charlie Chaplin	Wolfgang Amadeus Mozart
Cesar Chavez	John Muir
Winston Churchill	Sir Isaac Newton
Cleopatra	Richard Nixon
Christopher Columbus	Georgia O'Keeffe
Hernando Cortes	Louis Pasteur
Marie Curie	Pablo Picasso
Amelia Earhart	Elvis Presley
Thomas Edison	Jackie Robinson
Albert Einstein	Norman Rockwell
Duke Ellington	Anwar Sadat
Dian Fossey	Margaret Sanger
Benjamin Franklin	Oskar Schindler
Galileo Galilei	John Steinbeck
Emma Goldman	Jim Thorpe
Jane Goodall	Mark Twain
Martha Graham	Queen Victoria
Stephen Hawking	Pancho Villa
Jim Henson	H. G. Wells

Jane Goodall

by
Paula Bryant Pratt

Lucent Books, P.O. Box 289011, San Diego, CA 92198-9011

Library of Congress Cataloging-in-Publication Data

Pratt, Paula, 1959–
    Jane Goodall / by Paula Bryant Pratt.
      p. cm.—(The Importance of)
    Includes bibliographical references (p.   ) and index.
    Summary: Examines the life of the woman primatologist
who did the first long-term study of chimpanzees in the wild
in Tanganyika, now Tanzania, Africa.
    ISBN 1-56006-082-4 (alk. pap.)
    1. Goodall, Jane, 1934–   —Juvenile literature.
2. Chimpanzees—Research—Juvenile literature.   3. Women
primatologists—England—Biography—Juvenile literature.
[1. Goodall, Jane, 1934– . 2. Chimpanzees. 3. Zoologists.
4. Women—Biography.]   I. Title. II. Series.
QL31.G58P735   1997
591'.092—dc20   96–15596
[B]   CIP
                                       AC

Copyright 1997 by Lucent Books, Inc., P.O. Box 289011,
San Diego, California, 92198-9011

Printed in the U.S.A.

Contents

Foreword   7

Important Dates in the Life of Jane Goodall   8

INTRODUCTION
A Lifelong Observer   9

CHAPTER 1
The Young Naturalist   11

CHAPTER 2
Into Africa   22

CHAPTER 3
The Work Begins   34

CHAPTER 4
Acceptance   44

CHAPTER 5
Establishing an Identity   53

CHAPTER 6
Gombe Blossoms   59

CHAPTER 7
Tragedy in Paradise   74

CHAPTER 8
Crusading for Conservation   84

CHAPTER 9
Jane Goodall's Influence   94

Notes   105

For Further Reading   107

Works Consulted   108

Index   109

Credits   111

About the Author   112

Foreword

THE IMPORTANCE OF biography series deals with individuals who have made a unique contribution to history. The editors of the series have deliberately chosen to cast a wide net and include people from all fields of endeavor. Individuals from politics, music, art, literature, philosophy, science, sports, and religion are all represented. In addition, the editors did not restrict the series to individuals whose accomplishments have helped change the course of history. Of necessity, this criterion would have eliminated many whose contribution was great, though limited. Charles Darwin, for example, was responsible for radically altering the scientific view of the natural history of the world. His achievements continue to impact the study of science today. Others, such as Chief Joseph of the Nez Percé, played a pivotal role in the history of their own people. While Joseph's influence does not extend much beyond the Nez Percé, his nonviolent resistance to white expansion and his continuing role in protecting his tribe and his homeland remain an inspiration to all.

These biographies are more than factual chronicles. Each volume attempts to emphasize an individual's contributions both in his or her own time and for posterity. For example, the voyages of Christopher Columbus opened the way to European colonization of the New World. Unquestionably, his encounter with the New World brought monumental changes to both Europe and the Americas in his day. Today, however, the broader impact of Columbus's voyages is being critically scrutinized. *Christopher Columbus,* as well as every biography in The Importance Of series, includes and evaluates the most recent scholarship available on each subject.

Each author includes a wide variety of primary and secondary source quotations to document and substantiate his or her work. All quotes are footnoted to show readers exactly how and where biographers derive their information, as well as provide stepping stones to further research. These quotations enliven the text by giving readers eyewitness views of the life and times of each individual covered in The Importance Of series.

Finally, each volume is enhanced by photographs, bibliographies, chronologies, and comprehensive indexes. For both the casual reader and the student engaged in research, The Importance Of biographies will be a fascinating adventure into the lives of people who have helped shape humanity's past and present, and who will continue to shape its future.

IMPORTANT DATES IN THE LIFE OF JANE GOODALL

1934

Jane Goodall is born on April 3.

1942

Goodall's parents divorce.

1952

Graduates from Uplands.

1957

Sails to Africa.

1960

Arrives at Gombe Stream Game Reserve.

1962

Begins first semester at Cambridge University; Baron Hugo van Lawick arrives at Gombe.

1963

Goodall receives National Geographic Society's Franklin Burr Award for Contribution to Science.

1964

Marries van Lawick; receives second Franklin Burr Award.

1965

Goodall receives doctorate in ethology from Cambridge; CBS television airs documentary "Miss Goodall and the Wild Chimpanzees."

1967

Son, Hugo Eric Louis (Grub), is born; Goodall publishes her first book, *My Friends the Wild Chimpanzees*.

1971

Publishes *In the Shadow of Man*.

1972

The Gombe chimpanzees break into two warring communities.

1974

Goodall and van Lawick divorce.

1975

Goodall marries Derek Bryceson; guerrilla fighters from Zaire kidnap and later release four of Goodall's students; two female chimpanzees begin cannibalizing infant chimpanzees.

1977

Goodall establishes the Jane Goodall Institute for Wildlife Research, Education and Conservation.

1980

Bryceson dies of cancer.

1986

Goodall publishes *The Chimpanzees of Gombe: Patterns of Behavior*; forms the Committee for the Conservation and Care of Chimpanzees.

1988

Publishes *My Life with the Chimpanzees*.

1990

Publishes *Through a Window: My Thirty Years with the Chimpanzees of Gombe*.

1991

Edinburgh Medal, honoring scientists who have made a contribution to the understanding and well-being of humanity, is awarded to Goodall.

1995

Receives Hubbard Medal, honoring distinction in exploration, discovery, and research, from National Geographic Society.

A Lifelong Observer

Before Jane Goodall began her long-term study of chimpanzees in the wild, few scientists believed that humans could get close enough to the apes to study them in their natural surroundings. In the more than thirty years since Goodall first set foot on the shores on Gombe Stream, Tanganyika, now Tanzania, Africa, that viewpoint has changed. Now primatologists, scientists who study primates other than recent humans, model their research on the pioneering methods of this courageous and determined woman.

Learning from the Chimpanzees

Jane Goodall came to the forests of Africa without a preconceived idea about what she had come to find out. She only wanted to watch, listen, and learn from the chimpanzees themselves. In an amazingly short time she got close enough to the chimpanzees to touch them. Soon she was recording startling discoveries: She observed chimpanzees fashioning tools out of twigs; she saw them hunt and share meat like humans do; she learned about their social groups and how individual chimpanzees rose to power or sank to outcast status. She saw them greet one another

Jane Goodall with her favorite subject, the chimpanzee. Goodall pioneered a type of animal research that consisted of hours of sitting, watching, and taking careful notes on animal behavior.

A chimpanzee uses a stick as a tool. This behavior was originally witnessed by Goodall.

like humans greet one another, with outstretched hands, hugs, and kisses. And she saw them commit acts of violence such as cannibalism and warfare on other members of their social group, just as people themselves have done.

That chimpanzees behave similarly to humans was an exciting discovery. It meant that there were other animals besides humans who could behave in ways once thought to belong solely to humans. Goodall's findings in her many years studying chimpanzees have challenged scientists to come up with a new definition for humans. Humans alone could no longer be called the toolmakers, for example, because chimpanzees were now seen to share this trait. Humans were no longer the only animals thought to reason out problems or think abstractly, because Goodall's research suggested that chimpanzees planned and thought as well.

Noticing which behaviors chimps cling to that humans have relinquished and which behaviors both species continue to share can shed light on what makes humans different from their ape relatives. This gives us an idea of what traits are unique to being human and what traits are shared between species. In Jane Goodall's search for meaning through acute observation, she has learned and shared much about chimpanzee behavior and the chimpanzee's place in the scheme of things. Thanks to Goodall, science has been able to understand more about the links between one species and another, between humans and their nearest relative, the wild ape. And also thanks to Goodall, people have learned more about their own place in the scheme of things, understanding perhaps a little more clearly what it means to be human.

1 The Young Naturalist

Five-year-old Jane was missing. Her worried mother had been searching for her for hours, unaware that Jane was close by—hiding out in the henhouse, spying on a chicken about to lay an egg. Jane had been curious about eggs for weeks. She wondered how in the world hens produced them. Since no one she asked seemed to know the answer, Jane decided to see for herself.

It was not easy. When she followed a clucking chicken into the henhouse, the bird squawked in alarm and scuttled away. Jane realized that she would have to wait inside the henhouse, hidden out of sight. Then when a hen decided it was ready to lay an egg, Jane would be ready too.

The henhouse was stuffy and dark, and the straw prickled Jane's bare legs as she crouched, waiting and watching. Finally a chicken strutted in and settled down in front of Jane's hiding place. It did not seem aware of Jane, who kept still as stone about five feet away, knowing that if she moved, the hen would startle. Slowly the hen raised itself from the straw and bent forward. A round, white egg slowly emerged from the feathers between her legs. The hen wiggled once, and the egg plopped onto the straw. Clucking loudly, the hen fluffed her feathers and nudged the egg with her beak, then strut-

ted away. Jane had waited hours, but she had at last witnessed the actual laying of an egg. Her patience and determination had paid off.

An Understanding Mother

Jane's muscles were stiff and sore as she jumped up and ran back to the house, calling excitedly to her mother, who was just about to telephone the police and report her daughter missing. In *My Life with the Chimpanzees*, Jane Goodall recalls the thrill of that day and her mother's reaction: "This was my first serious observation of animal behavior. . . . How lucky I was that I had an understanding mother! Instead of being angry because I had given her a scare, she wanted to know all about the wonderful thing I had just seen."[1]

Jane Goodall, the five-year-old child who knew the value of watching and waiting, grew up to become a world-famous ethologist, a scientist who studies animal behavior in the wild. How did her traditional upbringing in a proper English family prepare her for a dangerous and groundbreaking scientific career? Her mother's warm support for her early explorations may have done much to nur-

What About the Fox?

Young Jane Goodall spent a lot of time with horses while growing up. One experience on horseback, detailed in her book My Life with the Chimpanzees, *changed the way she saw a traditional English sport forever.*

"Once I went fox hunting. I'd never thought about what that really meant before. I'd just imagined the excitement of jumping great hedges, the challenge of trying to keep up with the best riders, and the thrilling sound of the hunting horn. I hadn't thought about the fox.

I kept up only too well. So I saw the fox dug up out of his den, where he had at last found safety (he thought), and I watched the huntsman throw the exhausted creature to the hounds to be torn up. Then I felt sick, and the excitement of the hunt was gone. I never went hunting again."

ture Jane's childhood dream of going to Africa to work with animals when she grew up.

A Hairy Friend

In fact, Jane was only a year old when her mother introduced her to a chimpanzee. This particular primate was a toy one, unlike the real apes Jane would work with as an adult. In her book *In the Shadow of Man*, Goodall fondly recalls her mother's unusual gift:

> When I was just over one year old my mother gave me a toy chimpanzee, a large hairy model celebrating the birth of the first chimpanzee infant ever born in the London Zoo. Most of my mother's friends were horrified and predicted that the ghastly creature would give a small child nightmares; but Jubilee (as the celebrated infant itself was named) was my most loved possession and accompanied me on all my childhood travels. I still have the worn old toy.[2]

Jane's mother, Margaret Myfanwe Joseph, was a novelist who wrote books under the name Vanne Goodall. Her husband, Mortimer Herbert Morris-Goodall, was an engineer whose hobby was race-car driving. Their daughter Jane was born April 3, 1934. Mortimer sometimes took his little girl out for drives in his fancy, expensive Aston Martin motorcar. Jane may have inherited her daring and love of adventure from her daredevil father, her creative thinking and appreciation of the continual dramas played out in nature from her writer mother. The Morris-Goodalls had another daughter, Judy, when Jane was three. They lived in a house just outside London, along with a bull terrier and the children's beloved caregiver, Nanny.

The Threat of War

When Jane was five and Judy was one, their parents decided it was time for a change. The family moved to France. The cultured Morris-Goodalls wanted their children to grow up speaking fluent French. However, 1939 was the wrong year to live in western Europe. Only a few months after the family sold their house in England and moved to France, Hitler began stirring up the political unrest that would soon lead to the outbreak of World War II. Realizing the danger they faced, Jane's parents hurried back to England with the girls. The family moved in temporarily with Mortimer's mother, who still lived in the centuries-old manor house where Jane's father had grown up.

The Manor House

The creepy old country estate stimulated five-year-old Jane's curiosity; its sights and smells urged her to explore. Made of stone, it had no central heating or electricity. Fragrant oil lamps lighted the chilly rooms at nightfall. Next door to the estate stretched a huge farm. Jane often watched the dairymaids milking cows, squirting the milk into a pail the old-fashioned way. Nearby sprawled the ruins of a castle that had belonged to Henry VIII in the sixteenth century. The crumbling stones housed spiderwebs and bats. Jane's grandmother loved geese and let them roam her lawn. Jane's Uncle Rex, her father's brother, ran a small horse-racing stable and racecourse about four miles from the manor house. Already, Jane was able to get a close look at many animals and birds.

But the family did not stay at the manor house long. When England declared war on Germany, Jane's father joined the army in the fight against Hitler. Not long afterward Nanny left the family to get married. Until Jane's father returned from the war, only Jane, her little sister, and her mother, called Vanne, were left. The three of them went to live with Vanne's mother and two sisters in a big brick house surrounded by tall hedges. The lovely home, called the Birches, was in the seaside town of Bournemouth, on the southern coast of England. Jane did the rest of her growing up in the English countryside, only a moment's jog from the beach with its pine-covered cliffs.

The Birches

The beach was Jane's playground, but even the backyard garden of her grandmother's home kept her constantly entertained by dozens of miniature dramas. A big, overgrown place surrounded by hedges that "shut out the world," as Jane recalled later, the garden was dominated by a beech tree that Jane did her homework in. She often stopped to watch and listen to the birds that shared her perch. She loved the tree so much that her grandmother gave it to her as a present for her tenth birthday.

In Hitler's Shadow

While Jane sought refuge in the comforting shelter of her natural surroundings, the outside world was exploding in conflict.

Inevitably the realities of war broke through the barricade of Jane's backyard paradise. Although the town was not a central target, more than one bomb dropped on Bournemouth. Jane's family built an air-raid shelter in the basement. When the air-raid whistle shrieked its warning, the family huddled together inside the cramped steel cage, waiting for an all clear signal to reassure them that they were safe for a while longer.

There were other daily reminders of war. Food was rationed, and each family was allowed tiny portions of candy, milk, and eggs. According to Goodall, adults usually gave most of their rations to their children. In addition, because American soldiers flowed through England on their way to the fronts in France, the Netherlands, and Belgium, American tanks and trucks lined the road leading to Jane's home. The Yankee soldiers often shared candy with Jane and the other local children.

Bombs, tanks, and rationing aside, Goodall and her sister were not upset by the danger brewing outside the family gar-

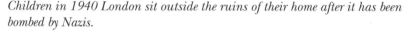

Children in 1940 London sit outside the ruins of their home after it has been bombed by Nazis.

den hedges. She writes: "At the beginning we were too young to understand what was going on; by the end we had become used to news of battles, defeats, and victories."[3] However, a desire to retreat from the turmoil going on around her may have shaped Jane's preferences for solitude and nature early on. There were no bombs and tanks in the animal world, although she would learn later that there was no shortage of violence.

Jane also escaped the outside world through reading. Her mother raised her to love books, saying that reading would help her forget her troubles whenever she felt sad. The house was filled with fascinating books from Vanne's childhood. Since the family could not afford to buy many new books during wartime, they made weekly trips to the local library.

Where the Wild Things Are

When Jane was seven, she encountered a book that she says sparked her decision to go to Africa someday—*The Story of Dr. Dolittle*, by Hugh Lofting. The children's classic recounts the fantasy adventures of a wonderful doctor who understands animal language. She read the book three times before it had to go back to the library—finishing it the last time through by flashlight under the bedsheets. Her grandmother bought Jane her own copy of *Dr. Dolittle* for Christmas so that she could reread it as often as she liked. Later Goodall said of the book's influence on her: "I wanted to come as close to talking to animals as I could—to be like Dr. Dolittle."[4]

Other borrowed books fed Jane's growing interest in animals, including *The Jungle Book*, by Rudyard Kipling, about a human boy raised by wolves. Perhaps she pictured herself in Mowgli's place. The Tarzan books, by Edgar Rice Burroughs, were also favorites. Jane also checked out library books on all types of wild animals the world over, whether wolves, bears, tapirs, or sloths.

The Comfort of Nature

Jane's dream of going to Africa and finding a home among the wild creatures was formed around the time of her parents' divorce, when she was eight years old. Mortimer moved into an apartment in London; Jane, Judy, and their mother, Vanne, stayed on at the Birches in Bournemouth. While she scarcely mentions the divorce in any of her books, Goodall may have sought comfort early in the idea of entering an exotic world far from family troubles and disappointments.

Jane's desire to escape civilization also showed in her attitude toward school. While she loved to read and got good grades, Jane was impatient with formal education. To someone who loved the freedom of the outdoors as much as she did, classrooms were too confining:

> I didn't mind the work—some of it I liked very much. But I hated having to leave home every morning, and I hated having to spend time indoors when I wanted to be outside. . . . I longed for the weekends when I could go horseback riding. Most of all I longed for the holidays. Then, for days on end, I was free from school bells and school regimentation.[5]

The Alligator Club

Jane's most important lessons were self-taught. She was learning all the time from the careful observations she made of the natural world around her. She could not go to Africa yet, or even to a zoo, since there was none nearby. So she watched the living things close to home instead. As a forum for her enthusiasm, Jane started the Alligator Club with her sister and two friends who came to stay with the Morris-Goodalls on most school vacations, Sally and Sue Cary. As club leader, Jane, known as Red Admiral, led Sally (Puffin), Sue (Ladybird), and Judy (Trout), in the nature-watching techniques she had picked up from her reading.

The club met in the garden, where the girls kept a trunk containing four mugs and a supply of cocoa. Their wartime feasts were thin, consisting only of bread crusts and biscuits, but they savored the privacy of their meetings. Often the four girls hiked along the cliffs or shore. Jane scrawled detailed notes. Back at the Birches they looked up the names of the insects or birds they had glimpsed. In the garden the Alligator Club fattened up pet snails in a bottomless box covered with a piece of glass. They moved the box to a fresh patch of lawn each time the snails ate all the grass inside the enclosure. After the snails dined, the girls lined them up and placed bets on which one would reach the end of a six-foot racetrack first.

One summer the Alligator Club put together its own natural history museum. The girls labeled their collection of pressed flowers and shells. They dangled a human skeleton from an uncle's medical school days. The older girls sent the younger ones out to attract visitors to the museum. After people toured the displays, they were asked to contribute to a society that put old horses safely out to pasture.

The Alligator Club had to disband each time school started up again. But it published its own magazine during the school year. Jane was the editor and usually the magazine's only contributor, even though the other members were invited to submit comments and suggestions. She filled each issue with her own nature notes and drawings.

When not occupied with the club, Jane kept learning from her motley collection of pets, including an assortment of earthworms that she kept under her pillow. Another time, while sick in bed, she coaxed a bird into her bedroom, and it built a nest in her bookshelf. However, she credits a pet dog named Rusty that she borrowed from neighbors with teaching her some of her most significant early lessons about animal behavior.

No Ordinary Hound

Rusty lived in a hotel around the corner from the Birches. He tagged along whenever Jane arrived to take a shop owner's collie, Budleigh, for its daily walk on the beach. Soon Rusty was outperforming Budleigh at tricks, like balancing a biscuit on the end of his nose, without benefit of a single lesson. Jane began taking a special interest in Rusty. In *My Life with the Chimpanzees*, she writes: "Rusty taught me so much about animal behavior, lessons I have remembered all my life. He taught me that dogs can think things out—that they can reason."[6]

Jane concluded that Rusty could reason because when she threw a ball out an upstairs window, he put together a series of actions—watching to see where it landed, running downstairs, and barking for an outside door to be opened—that suggested that he had planned a strategy for retrieving the ball. She was also fascinated by the way he sulked when she scolded him for pushing open a door with muddy paws, when she had earlier praised him for pushing open the same door when his paws were clean. Jane found the sulking almost human, as if Rusty possessed something similar to a "sense of justice," as she put it. The hours of time she spent watching and training Rusty were just as valuable to her as any lesson she learned in school, Jane felt.

Despite her lack of enthusiasm for the dreary school routine, Jane came in second or third in her class at the end of each term. She recalls that her best friend, Marie-Claude Mange—known as Clo—was

Stopping the Torment

Jane Goodall's later activism for animal rights may have been partly motivated by this childhood memory from her book My Life with the Chimpanzees. *She compares her reaction to the tormenting of some crabs with the reaction of her son, nicknamed Grub, to a similar incident.*

"It is really important for animals that we speak our minds when we see something wrong. And that is not always easy. When I was [young] I once saw four boys, much bigger than I was, pulling the legs off crabs. I was very upset. I asked them why they did it, and they said, 'None of your business.' I told them it was cruel. They laughed. And I went away. Now, forty years later, I am still ashamed of myself. Why didn't I try harder to stop them from tormenting those crabs?

I was not like my son. Once, when he was five years old, he was at a nursery school in California (at a time when I used to teach, one quarter a year, at Stanford University). One day he saw a seven-year-old boy hosing a terrified rabbit in its cage and laughing. Grub went up and tried to pull the hose away. The boy wouldn't let go, so Grub started a fight. And though he was much smaller, he managed to win.

The teacher was very angry with Grub and punished him. She didn't even punish the other boy for being cruel. But Grub, even though he was punished, knew he had done the right thing. He had stopped the tormenting of the rabbit."

either just above or just below her. However, Jane graduated with honors from the Uplands private school at Parkstone, near Bournemouth, at eighteen.

Jane wanted to go on to college, perhaps to Oxford University. However, Vanne could not afford to pay her tuition unless she received a large scholarship. In order to win a scholarship, applicants needed to be proficient in a foreign language. Unfortunately Jane had struggled in school with both foreign languages and math, excelling in biology, English, and history.

Instead of going on to college, Jane visited Germany. With World War II over, Vanne wanted her to realize that not all Germans thought like the Nazis. Jane also hoped to pick up some German there and perhaps improve her chances of winning a college scholarship. But the German family she stayed with was anxious to improve their English. They refused to speak to her in German, and she picked up only a few words. However, Jane saw something during her four-month stay that moved her deeply:

> I went on a visit to the city of Cologne. Like so many other German cities, it had been heavily bombed by Allied forces during the war. As you looked out across the flattened, battered city, you could see the spire of Cologne Cathedral. It rose, quite undamaged, from the rubble of the surrounding buildings. To me it seemed like a message from God, telling us that however bad things may seem, in the end, goodness will win. . . . Seeing the spire of Cologne Cathedral that day meant more to me than all the sermons I had ever listened to.[7]

Secretaries Work Anywhere

Acting on the advice of her mother, who said that secretaries could get jobs anywhere in the world, Jane enrolled in a London secretarial school, learning typing, shorthand, and bookkeeping. In London she visited art galleries, went to concerts, and accepted dinner and theater dates from young men: "I had never had time for boys before; I had been far too busy with horses and walking in the country and Rusty. But now I . . . was out in the big world."[8] London was a far cry from Africa, but Jane had not forgotten her dream. Perhaps a secretarial job would provide the stepping-stone to something more exciting later on, she hoped.

After she received her secretarial school diploma, Jane's first job was at her Aunt Olly's clinic in Bournemouth. Olly worked with children who had birth defects. Jane typed the clinic's correspondence. Goodall writes that, in the process, she learned much about courage and determination:

> I learned so much at that clinic. Ever since then, when things have gone wrong in my life, I remember how lucky I am to be healthy. I thank God for that, and I feel more determined to solve my problems or get over my sadness. . . . And I feel a special closeness with people who are . . . disabled in any way.[9]

On the River

Jane's next job was at Oxford University, the school she had once hoped to attend.

Goodall found inspiration in the spires of Cologne's cathedral, rising out of the rubble of World War II Germany.

After putting in her tedious hours as a file clerk, she was free to socialize with the students. She also polished athletic skills that she would later use in Africa—canoeing and punting. While paddling her canoe silently along the river, she noticed the behaviors of moorhens, kingfishers, and families of swans defending their young. Punting was less graceful than canoeing, since it involved shoving a flat-bottomed boat along by sticking a long pole into the river bottom. Beginners often tumbled from their seats into the water after they clung to their poles when they stuck in the mud. Soon Jane was a master at the difficult hand-over-hand punting technique.

After a year at Oxford, Jane returned to London. She moved in with her father, welcoming the opportunity to get to know him better. During the next year she worked at a job she loved—selecting background music for a documentary film company. She also learned about editing film and mixing sound tracks. It was fascinating work but paid little. Part of her plan was to put money aside toward her goal of going to Africa. But Jane found it almost impossible to save much money in London, where there were so many things to see and do. However, she never forgot her ultimate goal. She kept her vision of the future alive by reading all she could about African wildlife and spending hours wandering through London's natural history museum.

Africa on the Horizon

A letter out of the blue from her old school friend from Uplands, Clo, made

Jane worked for a year at Oxford University as a file clerk. To keep her dream of going to Africa alive, Goodall worked on athletic skills that she would later need in Africa.

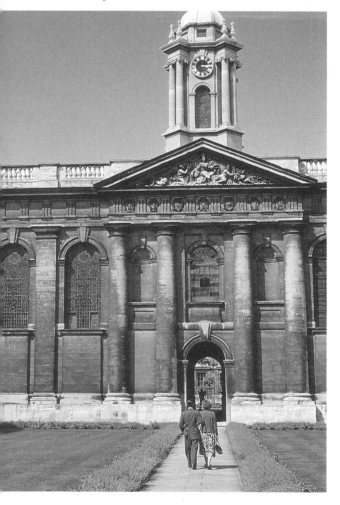

Jane's distant vision zoom into sharp focus. Clo wrote that her parents had just bought a farm in Kenya, Africa. She invited Jane to visit her there. Jane accepted immediately. However, there was still the matter of paying for the long trip.

Now that Africa was glistening on the horizon, Jane's plans accelerated. Although she loved the work, she quit the low-paying job with the film studio and left London to return to Bournemouth, where the cost of living was cheaper. Back at the Birches with her mother and aunts, Jane took a job as a waitress at a big hotel just around the block. The work was not easy. Jane had to master new skills that were not taught in secretarial school, such as balancing on one hand a stack of thirteen plates piled high with food. She must have learned well, for within four months of waitressing, she had amassed enough wages and tips for a round-trip fare to Africa.

When she boarded the *Kenya Castle* passenger liner in 1957, Jane Goodall was twenty-three years old. Mere chance had not brought her on board, but hard work, patience, and determination. It would not be the first time she would make use of these qualities.

No Girl Can Do That

Clearly, Jane demonstrated while still young the traits that would help her succeed in her adult career—keen powers of observation, patience, and an ability to identify with animals. She needed to nurture these traits early in life because when she was young, women did not move to Africa to start careers. Jane's guidance counselor at Uplands had discouraged her from her

Learning to Curtsy

"I went to a couple of the famous May balls at Oxford. My first ball gown was white net, with pale gray swan feathers scattered over it, each one kept in place with a sequin. It was very expensive originally, but had been worn by a model in a fashion show, so I got it very cheap indeed. I felt like a princess when I wore that gown.

I remember one other dress—a wonderful crimson red lace. I am sure my mother did without cinemas and all sorts of other things in order to buy it for me. It had to be a good dress, for Uncle Michael and Auntie Joan were going to present me to Queen Elizabeth in Buckingham Palace. First I had to learn a full state curtsy. I had lessons from a funny old lady. She told me to practice and practice, always balancing something on my head. So I was quite proficient by the time I curtsied to the queen and Prince Philip. It was a magnificent occasion."

goal, saying that no girl could do what Jane dreamed of doing. But Jane's mother had brought her up never to take no for an answer. Even Jane's uncle had doubted her, according to writer Sy Montgomery:

Once Jane, hiding in a tree, overheard her mother telling her uncle about Jane's plans. "She doesn't have the stamina," her uncle said. Jane had begun to suffer migraines [headaches] when she started school, but from that day forward, Jane never again complained of migraines.[10]

Jane instinctively was drawn toward a future career that few young women before her had ever thought possible for themselves. Her natural qualities propelled her toward that dream, although she could not yet know the ultimate importance—both to science and to women in science—of the groundbreaking work she would pioneer in the wilds of Africa.

2 Into Africa

Most of the other passengers aboard the *Kenya Castle* huddled in their cabins when the ocean got choppy, fighting off seasickness. Twenty-three-year-old Jane Goodall was often the only passenger left on deck. Too excited to feel queasy, she caught glimpses of dolphins, sharks, and flying fish from her shipboard vantage point. She wanted the trip to go on forever, but she knew that even more exciting sights were still ahead on shore. Twenty-one days after leaving London, Goodall disembarked at the port town of Mombasa, Kenya, on the East African coast and boarded a train for the two-day journey to the capital city of Nairobi.

Experiencing Africa Up Close

Clo Mange picked up her friend in Nairobi. On the drive to Clo's family farm in the White Highlands of Kenya, Goodall saw her first African animal, a giraffe, up close:

> He stood on his long legs in the middle of the dirt road, his long neck towering above the car, and looked down his long nose at us. His beautiful dark eyes were fringed with long lashes. He was chewing acacia thorns, and I could see that his long tongue was almost black. Finally he turned and cantered away. It looked as though he ran in slow motion.[11]

Meeting up with that gentle, otherworldly beast truly convinced Goodall that she had finally reached the land of her lifelong dreams. Now it was up to her to begin the hard work of taking hold of that fantasy and turning it into a reality that she could participate in.

Goodall visited with Clo and her family for three weeks. Then she felt it was time to venture out on her own. Clo had already helped her friend arrange for a secretarial job with a British corporation that had a branch in Nairobi. Goodall wanted to earn her own money while looking for a job that would allow her to work with animals. She rented an apartment in Nairobi. As she worked at the boring tasks before her, she constantly kept her eyes and ears open for information that would lead her to the work she really wanted.

Finding a Lead

Once again keeping a receptive mind paid off. After two months in Nairobi, Goodall

Louis and Mary Leakey work in the field. Leakey helped Goodall fulfill her desire to study in Africa.

heard about Louis Leakey, whom she calls in *My Life with the Chimpanzees* the man who made her dreams come true. Leakey was the director of the Coryndon Memorial Museum of Natural History in Nairobi. He was a paleontologist, a scientist who studies the past by examining ancient bones and fossils. Leakey, already well known, would soon become famous for discovering with the aid of his wife, Mary, the pieces of two fossilized skeletons of prehistoric humans in 1959 and 1960. But by the time Jane Goodall traveled to Africa in 1957, Leakey's interests were already shifting from studying fossils to studying living animals. He believed that learning about the behavior of apes, humankind's closest relatives, would allow scientists to shed light on the behavior of prehistoric humans and how they had developed. Many of his colleagues did not share his enthusiasm for the idea that apes and people might behave in similar ways.

Thus, when Goodall heard about Louis Leakey, he was already interested in animal behavior. However, when Goodall telephoned the museum and asked to speak with Dr. Leakey about a job, he did not sound encouraging. Gruffly, Leakey identified himself and growled, "What do you want?"

Undaunted, Goodall made an appointment and showed up at his office. She recalls it as "big [and] untidy . . . strewn with papers, fossil bones, teeth, stone tools, and all kinds of other things—including a big cage in which lived a minute mouse with her six babies."[12]

On the Road to a New Career

Unlike his telephone voice, Leakey was friendly in person and as big and untidy as his office. In his fifties, he walked with a cane, his head jutting forward above his paunchy stomach. His long white hair flopped messily over his forehead. Goodall had stored up a huge amount of facts about African animals from her

Living, Breathing Animals

Soon after she was hired by paleontologist Louis Leakey as his assistant, the young Jane Goodall was asked to join him and his wife on one of their famous digs at Olduvai Gorge in Africa. The trip was Jane's first experience in the African wilderness. In her book In the Shadow of Man, *she recalls her encounters with animals, both alive and fossilized.*

"The digging itself was fascinating. For hours, as I picked away at the ancient clay or rock of the Olduvai fault to extract the remains of creatures that had lived millions of years ago, the task would be purely routine, but from time to time, and without warning, I would be filled with awe by the sight or the feel of some bone I held in my hand. This—this very bone—had once been part of a living, breathing animal that had walked and slept and propagated [reproduced] its species. What had it really looked like? What color was its hair; what was the odor of its body?

It was the evenings, however, that gave those few months their special enchantment for me. . . . Olduvai in the dry season becomes almost a desert, but as [the other assistant, Gillian, and I] walked past the low thorn-bushes we often glimpsed dik-diks, those graceful miniature antelopes scarcely larger than a hare. Sometimes there would be a small herd of gazelles or giraffes, and on a few memorable occasions we saw a black rhinoceros plodding along the gorge below. Once we came face to face with a young male lion: he was no more than forty feet away when we heard his soft growl and peered around to see him on the other side of a small bush. . . . Slowly we backed away while he watched, his tail twitching. Then . . . he followed us as we walked deliberately across the gorge toward the open, treeless plains on the other side. As we began to climb upward he vanished into the vegetation and we did not see him again."

reading, and her knowledge impressed Leakey, she felt sure. Leakey respected this slender and intelligent young woman. His secretary had just quit, so he was more than willing to sign Jane Goodall on then and there as his assistant. Her career with animals had begun.

The man who would direct Goodall toward the study of chimpanzees was a complex person. Leakey was in constant motion, despite an arthritic hip, talking a mile a minute. His theories were often dramatic, based on conclusions that he drew before he had gathered enough data to back them up. Nevertheless, his wild ideas about prehistoric humans often proved correct, to the irritation of his more conservative colleagues.

Persistence and Intuition

In fact, Leakey's professors at Cambridge University had laughed at his plans to search Africa for the remains of prehistoric humans, for most paleontologists believed that humans originated in Asia or Europe. But Leakey seemed to have a second sense that drew him like a magnet to the right place at the right time. Yet, without persistence to go along with that intuition, he may never have found the evidence of early civilization that he was seeking. It took him nearly thirty years of digging for fossils before he and Mary Leakey unearthed the famous skeletal fragments of *Zinjanthropus* and *Homo habilis.* The first set of remains proved that humans were twice as ancient as people had previously thought. The second discovery, the remains of a prehistoric child, was thought to be the direct ancestor of humans today.

Because Leakey often made his discoveries through playful exploration and following up on hunches, he tended to look for the same type of creative thinking in the people he worked with. Leakey often screened applicants by testing them with a deck of playing cards, asking them to recall which were red and which were black. Winning applicants also noticed that some of the cards were slightly bent. The point of such tests was to satisfy Leakey that his potential employees had strong powers of observation, a quality he considered all-important in the field.

The Leakeys hold a jaw from a newly discovered skull. The Leakeys' work on the origins of humans proved the human species was much older than scientists had previously thought.

Leakey's Views on Women

Leakey's colleagues were quick to notice that he preferred to hire women to carry out his animal research projects. Leakey made no secret of his belief that women were more perceptive than men. He also found women tougher, with greater stick-to-itiveness than men. Leakey believed in detailed, long-term studies of animal behavior. He was contemptuous of scientists who were willing to devote only a few months to the research side of their careers. According to Sy Montgomery: "Louis believed that women were particularly well suited to long-term studies. Both biology and society encourage women to invest their time in long-term projects, he pointed out: raising a child to adulthood, for instance, demands two decades of commitment."[13]

Digging for Answers

Goodall's first assignment was to accompany the Leakeys and another female assistant on an archaeological dig at Olduvai Gorge in Tanganyika. This was the secluded site where the Leakeys would eventually make their famous discoveries. Under the scorching sun the work was painstaking, backbreaking, and at times hair-raising—at one point Goodall and Mary Leakey encountered a curious leopard. Goodall helped Mary Leakey dig away at the hard topsoil with a pickax to unearth layers of fossils hidden below: "I was strong and very healthy, and I offered to help her. We got on well together, sweating away as we swung the heavy implements."[14]

Jane Goodall spent three months at Olduvai with Louis and Mary Leakey. She was blissfully happy to be out in the African wilderness at last. At night around the campfire the group often heard the distant roar of lions or the high laughter of hyenas.

Louis Leakey was well aware of Goodall's affinity for animals and her preference for working with living creatures over decaying fossils. Toward the end of their three-month stay at Olduvai, Leakey

Goodall's first assignment with Leakey was at an archaeological dig at Olduvai Gorge (pictured).

first approached Goodall with an exciting idea. He told her that a group of chimpanzees lived in an isolated, rugged, mountainous area far from civilization on the shores of Lake Tanganyika—a place called the Gombe Stream Game Reserve. The reserve had been set aside by the British government in 1923 as a refuge for wild apes. Few studies of chimpanzees had ever been attempted, Leakey explained. Chimpanzees can be found only in Africa, and only one man, Henry W. Nissen, had tried to study their behavior in the wild because they were so difficult to find and follow. Leakey was particularly interested in the chimpanzees by the lake, he told her, because the fossil remains of prehistoric people were often found on the shores of lakes. Perhaps a study of chimpanzee behavior would reveal some details about the way our ancient ancestors might have lived under similar conditions, Leakey speculated. It would have to be a lengthy study, he added. Professor Nissen had managed to stay in the wild for only two months before giving up.

"A Sympathetic Understanding of Animals"

Leakey stressed that whoever went to the remote lakeshore to study the chimpanzees would have to have great patience and dedication. Goodall was hungry to tackle the job herself, but she knew that the researchers who usually conducted such studies had scientific training that she lacked. Louis Leakey let the matter go, but he often brought up the chimpanzee study after the expedition's return to Kenya. Goodall continued her work at the

museum, pondering her career options. One day she confronted Leakey and told him that she wanted to conduct the chimpanzee study. Leakey broke into a grin and asked what had taken her so long to come forward. He had wanted Goodall to go to Gombe all along.

When Goodall confided her fear that she lacked the proper qualifications, Leakey hastened to reassure her. According to Goodall's *In the Shadow of Man*: "He wanted someone with a mind uncluttered and unbiased by theory who would make the study for no other reason than a real desire for knowledge; and, in addition, someone with a sympathetic understanding of animals."[15]

Delayed Plans

Goodall knew that she was that person, even after Leakey explained that the project would take at least two years. Before the chimpanzee project could actually get underway, however, tangles of red tape had to be unraveled. These preparations took three years, pushing the start of the project up to 1960. The first thing Leakey had to do was raise the money to fund the project. This meant that he had to convince a wealthy contributor of the importance of the study. He also had to explain why he had chosen a young woman with little formal scientific training to head the study. Many of his colleagues were frank about their view that the eccentric fellow had finally gone off his rocker.

Eventually, however, Leighton Wilkie of the Wilkie Foundation in Des Plaines, Illinois, agreed to contribute enough money to cover a small boat, a tent, and airfare, as

In preparation for her trip to study chimpanzees, Goodall spent hours at the London Zoo (pictured), carefully observing captive chimps.

well as money to finance Goodall's first six months in the field. It was enough to get Goodall's research going.

Chimpanzees in London

During the fund-raising Leakey had sent Goodall back to England to learn all she could about chimpanzees. Since wild chimps were found only in Africa, she studied the apes who were living experimentally in researchers' homes, as well as chimpanzees in captivity at the London Zoo and the Royal Free Hospital. Through her extensive reading and observation, Goodall gained a growing respect for the primates. Chimpanzees were highly intelligent creatures, she learned, more like human beings than any other animal. Her anticipation mounted as she considered how lucky she was to be work-

ing with these particular animals out of all the others she could have chosen.

While in England awaiting the start of her fieldwork, Goodall worked as a film librarian for Granada Television, a company that was filming animal documentaries in the London Zoo. During her time off she spent hours watching the zoo's chimps. To her dismay she saw that the only male chimpanzee, called Dick, had been cooped up for so long in his tiny cage that he seemed insane. Crouched in a corner for hours at a time, Dick opened and closed his mouth and appeared to count his fingers—over and over. Goodall's heart went out to the magnificent creature who had become pathetic in his isolation.

After Leakey had completed the agreement with the Wilkie Foundation, he summoned Goodall back to Africa. However, she was not to come alone, he told her. Leakey had wangled approval for Goodall's project from the British government officials in Tanganyika. The cautious officials would allow Goodall to live and work in the remote area, but with one catch. They would not tolerate her entrance into the wilderness alone. A solitary woman, especially a white woman, roaming the wilds of Africa unprotected was unheard-of.

When Leakey told her that she would have to bring a companion, Goodall invited her mother. Vanne had already visited her daughter in Africa. She was thrilled by the prospect of a return visit. Vanne agreed to tag along for the first few months of the study. After that, they hoped that the officials would relax their rule and let Goodall stay on by herself.

Goodall and her mother flew to Nairobi, where Louis Leakey put them up in a hotel. There they gathered the supplies they would need for the expedition to Lake Tanganyika's Gombe Stream Game Reserve, where the chimpanzees Goodall would be studying ranged. They packed tents, bedding, pots and pans, and canned food. Goodall bought drab clothing in shades of green and brown so that she would blend in with the surrounding forest. She packed binoculars and stacks of notebooks for recording what she would see.

Just as it seemed the trip would finally get under way, Leakey received a telegram from the district commissioner of the

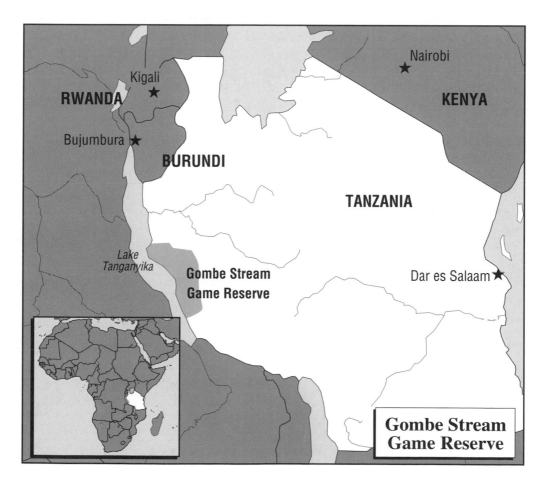

Kigoma region, where the Gombe reserve was located. African fishermen were fighting among themselves on the beaches of the chimpanzee reserve over who would fish from which beach. The unrest made it too dangerous for Goodall to begin her work, the commissioner felt. He insisted that they delay their plans until the game ranger for the area had time to sort things out.

To Goodall, poised on the brink of adventure, the setback was bitter. Leakey suggested a way for her to take her mind off the disappointment and use the delay constructively. Within a week Goodall, her mother, and two African guides were on their way to Lolui Island in the middle of Lake Victoria. On this unpopulated island Goodall would begin a three-week trial study of vervet monkeys living there. This

The Crocodile Poacher

While waiting to begin her chimpanzee research, Goodall spent three weeks on an island in the middle of Lake Victoria studying monkeys. She was on the lookout for dangerous wild animals, but an encounter with a crocodile poacher proved even more threatening, as she describes in My Life with the Chimpanzees.

"When I finally saw what was approaching, my heart gave a great thump. It was much more frightening than any hippo. It was an African, dressed only in a loincloth, with a spear in one hand. I knew at once that he was one of the crocodile poachers that Hassan [her guide] had told me about. And I knew that he could not fail to see me as he passed.

So I stepped out . . . and said, 'Jambo'—'How are you?' The man stopped as if I had hit him and, quick as lightning, raised his arm. The tip of the spear was pointed directly toward me. He seemed ready to impale me. But suddenly, perhaps because he saw I was just a white girl, he lowered his spear. . . . He shouted at me. I couldn't understand all he said, but I did gather that he would kill me if he saw me there again. . . .

I didn't feel like watching monkeys anymore that day. I . . . signaled for Hassan. . . . He immediately rowed around the island to the poachers' camp and talked to them. Finally they said they would leave me alone if I kept to my part of the island and never went near their camp. I was ready enough to stick to this arrangement. But I never really trusted them, and whenever I went after the monkeys . . . I was always expecting to see a sinister human shape lurking there."

When her chimpanzee study was unexpectedly delayed, Goodall used the time to study the vervet monkey.

preliminary work would prepare her for working with the chimps at Gombe. According to Goodall:

> The short study of the troop of monkeys taught me a good deal about such things as note-taking in the field, the sort of clothes to wear, the movements a wild monkey will tolerate in a human observer and those it will not. . . . I was sorry, in a way, when the expected message came one evening [recalling them to Nairobi], for it meant leaving the vervets just as I was beginning to learn about their behavior, just as I had become familiar with the different individuals of the troop. It is never easy to leave a job unfinished.[16]

Already, Goodall was exhibiting her uniquely personal way of doing research. She was not only patient and thorough. She also saw her subjects as individuals, not as mere statistics. Her natural warmth and empathy became a part of her work—completely different from the unemotional approach of most of her colleagues.

Goodall knew that her methods were different from those of the typical ethologist, but Leakey had assured her that her difference would be her strength. Goodall returned to Nairobi eager to start work. In only a few days Goodall and Vanne piled themselves and their gear into a Land Rover headed for Gombe. Dr. Bernard Verdcourt, the director of the East African Herbarium, had agreed to drive the women to their destination, planning to collect rare plant specimens on the way.

Riots in the Congo

It was an eight-hundred-mile drive over rough roads from Nairobi through Tanganyika to Kigoma. When the three travelers reached Kigoma, the town nearest to the Gombe Stream Game Reserve, chaos greeted them. Kigoma was in an uproar because riots had broken out in the Congo, now Zaire, about twenty-five miles west across Lake Tanganyika. Boatloads of

Belgian refugees from the bloodshed had crowded the beaches of Kigoma, seeking aid. The district commissioner advised Goodall's group to stay at a Kigoma hotel until it was certain that the riots would not spread.

Goodall, her mother, and Bernard Verdcourt booked rooms in a local hotel, but soon the hotel overflowed with homeless Belgians. Other refugees slept on cement floors in warehouses. On their second evening in Kigoma, Vanne, Verdcourt, and Goodall volunteered to help feed the homeless refugees, making mountains of sandwiches and handing them out along with fruit, chocolate, and cigarettes. Two nights later all the refugees had vanished aboard trains that would take them to Dar es Salaam, Tanganyika's capital city. The flurry of activity was over, but the party was still not allowed to set up camp at the chimpanzee reserve. The game ranger had not yet given them the go-ahead.

Gombe at Last

Finally, after another week, Goodall was given official permission to proceed to Gombe Stream Game Reserve. Money troubles, local squabbles, and political upheaval had set up roadblocks in her path so often that Goodall could hardly believe that she was finally free to start her research. In her book *In the Shadow of Man*, she described her feelings as the government launch steamed out of Kigoma harbor toward the northern shore of Lake Tanganyika:

By this time I had almost given up hope of ever seeing a chimpanzee; I had convinced myself that at any minute we would be ordered back to Nairobi. . . . [The] expedition had taken on a dreamlike quality. As the engine sprang to life and the anchor was drawn, we waved goodbye to Bernard. . . . I can remember looking down into the incredibly clear water and thinking to myself, I expect the boat will sink, or I shall fall overboard and be eaten by a crocodile. But good luck was with us.[17]

In *Watching the Wild Apes* writer Bettyann Kevles describes how the area that was soon to become famous as the site of Jane Goodall's chimpanzee research appeared on Goodall's arrival in July 1960:

Clear water lapped the shady shores of Lake Tanganyika where the baboons congregated, protected by game scouts in the Gombe Stream Reserve. . . . Fishing boats clung to the shores, wary of sudden winds that could raise whitecaps, making the freshwater lake seem like an ocean. Beyond the beach at Gombe, the shoreline zigzagged through rocky coves until sixteen miles to the south the port town of Kigoma thrust quays and jetties into the waters. Kigoma's shops, post office, and telegraph linked Gombe with the rest of Tanzania. Northward along the eastern shore . . . were the new nations of Burundi and Rwanda. And to the west, thirty miles across the lake, the Belgian Congo was just becoming the independent nation of Zaire.[18]

Gombe itself is part of the remaining primeval, or ancient, forest that once stretched across all of central Africa. The chimpanzees of Gombe share their lush rain forest with wild bushpigs, baboons, snakes, buffalo, and leopards. Streams course through the hilly terrain and tumble into the mirrorlike lake. Small fishing villages nestle along the shoreline, clusters of huts made up of mud and grass.

A Home Among the Wild Things

Goodall and Vanne were accompanied by a guide named David Anstey, who would introduce them to the local Africans. When Vanne first caught sight of the rugged shoreline of Gombe, she was worried by the steep slopes and the thickly forested valleys that seemed impossible to hike through. But Goodall's mother kept her concern to herself. Anstey, too, was worried. He told Goodall several months later that he had figured she would be ready to go home after only a few weeks.

But Goodall did not experience the same doubts. For her the arrival at her long-awaited destination still seemed very much like a dream.

Goodall left her companions after their camp had been organized for a quick walk up one of the steep slopes as if to re-assure herself that Gombe was, in fact, real. On that exploratory outing she watched a troop of baboons pass by and startled a white-tailed red-gold bushbuck, a type of antelope. Goodall recalls the peaceful sense of belonging that her solitary hike brought her: "I only stayed out on the mountain about three-quarters of an hour, but when I returned . . . I no longer felt an intruder. That night I pulled my camp bed into the open and slept with the stars above me twinkling down through the rustling fronds of a palm tree."[19]

After that peaceful night under the stars, Goodall felt a sense of union with the natural world. In the years to come she would often seek again that feeling of oneness in Gombe, out in the open among the creatures of the wilderness.

3 The Work Begins

Studying ape behavior to learn more about human behavior was not a new idea. Researchers before Jane Goodall had studied primates. But these researchers, such as Clarence Ray Carpenter, who studied rhesus monkeys in the 1930s, often experimented with and manipulated the animals they observed. For example, they implanted electrodes in the monkeys' brains or removed dominant males to see how the rest of the group would react. Later scientists such as Vernon Reynolds and Henry Nissen wanted to observe chimpanzee behavior without interfering with it the way Carpenter had. But they found their work impossible to continue. Nissen was forced to hide behind bushes in order to watch the primates without disturbing them, but the camouflage only ended up blocking his view.

Depressing Predictions

When other scientists had given up their studies in frustration, how could Goodall hope to succeed? According to writer Sy Montgomery: "Before leaving for Gombe, Jane had spoken with wildlife researchers in both Nairobi and London, and they all said she should not get her hopes up. The chimps would never get used to human observers." [20]

Despite such depressing predictions, Goodall's hopes were high. However, her first hurdle would be to shake the African guides that Kigoma officials had insisted on assigning to her. Goodall wanted to explore Gombe Stream alone, feeling that a single observer would be less likely to frighten the chimpanzees than a crowd of intruders would. However, local Africans had spread the rumor that the young British woman must be a government spy. They found it hard to believe she had come all the way to Africa just to watch apes. In addition, residents hoped someday to reclaim the Gombe Stream area for themselves. Because the area had been set aside as a protected game reserve, the locals were prohibited from hunting and settling in the desirable location. If Goodall said that she counted more chimps than were really there, she could cheat them out of their chance to get their fishing area back, they reasoned.

To keep an eye on her, the son of the chief of a nearby village insisted on coming along with Goodall on her first day out. To her relief, however, the young man immediately dropped the idea when she showed him the steep, thickly forested slopes she planned to climb:

Close Calls

In her early days at Gombe, Jane Goodall exposed herself to the risk of attack from other wild animals as she sat patiently watching for chimpanzees. This excerpt is from her book My Life with the Chimpanzees.

"Once, as I arrived on the Peak in the early morning before it was properly light, I saw the dark shape of a large animal looming in front of me. . . . My heart began to beat fast, for I realized it was a buffalo. Many hunters fear buffalo more than lions or elephants.

By a lucky chance the wind was blowing from him to me, so he couldn't smell me. He was peacefully gazing in the opposite direction and chewing his cud. He hadn't heard my approach. . . . Very slowly I retreated.

Another time, as I was sitting on the Peak, I heard a strange mewing sound. I looked around and there, about fifteen yards away, a leopard was approaching. I could just see the black and white tip of his tail above the tall grass. It was walking along the little trail that led directly to where I sat.

Leopards are not usually dangerous unless they have been wounded. But I was frightened of them in those days. . . . And so, very silently, I moved away and looked for chimps in another valley.

Later I went back to the Peak. I found that, just like any cat, that leopard had been very curious. There, in the exact place where I had been sitting, he had left his mark—his droppings."

A few minutes later he . . . told me he felt rather unwell and would not go with me that day. Later I found out he had expected that I would merely ride up and down the lakeshore in a boat, counting any chimpanzees I saw. The idea of clambering about in the mountains did not appeal to him at all, and I never saw him again.[21]

For the first few months, however, Goodall got used to the company of one or two local guides during her daily hikes. In addition to helping her carry supplies, they taught her a few things that would make her job easier: how to find the trails that pigs and baboons had already beaten through the underbrush so that she did not have to break new paths, how to cross streams, and how to recognize the red and orange fruit of the msulula trees where the chimps gathered to feed. Later on the officials at Kigoma would relax and no longer require her to travel with a guide.

Goodall stands outside a tent at her camp at Gombe Stream. It took her several months to get close to the chimps.

First Observations

During her first few months at Gombe, Goodall sighted chimpanzees daily, but fleetingly and from a distance. Armed with binoculars, she trudged through the thick undergrowth of valleys, waded through streams, and hiked mountain slopes, listening for the chimpanzees' hooting calls. These hoots signaled that the chimps had found a ripe fruit tree to feed on. From five hundred yards away—as close as she could come before the chimpanzees ran from her—Goodall spotted groups of chimps shinnying up tree trunks. But their movements in the trees were obscured by leaves. She could only guess at what they might be doing. Still, she continued to rise every morning before dawn, bid good-bye to Vanne at their camp, and roam the forest slopes and canyons in search of the elusive creatures. Her patience and determination had brought her to Gombe, and they would keep her there until she had accomplished her mission.

Three months into her six-month trial period, Goodall had not gotten any closer to the chimps. She began to feel pressured to observe more than just glimpses of them among the leaves. Montgomery quotes from a discouraged letter she wrote to Louis Leakey. Because he had demonstrated a fatherly affection for her, she had begun calling him her Fairy Foster Father, and he referred to her as his Foster Child: "Life is depressing—wet,

Goodall, holding binoculars, climbs a tree to get a better look at chimpanzees nearby. Goodall's persistence and patience paid off when the chimps began to let her get closer to them.

chimpless, and it seems impecunious [poor]. Fruit not fruiting. Chimps vanishing. Me being ill. Oh, just—everything." She signed off, "A despondent and sad FC [Foster Child]." [22]

The Fever

The illness Goodall referred to was malaria. A Kigoma doctor had assured Goodall and her mother that there was no malaria in Gombe, so they had brought no medication for the fever. Yet during that third month both Goodall and Vanne contracted the dangerous illness. For two weeks they lay on their camp beds in the hot, stuffy tent, sweating with fever. Vanne's temperature soared to 105 degrees every day. Dominic, their cook, urged them to see the doctor in Kigoma, but mother and daughter protested that they felt too ill to undergo the three-hour boat ride into town. So Dominic nursed them back to health. He checked on his patients several times each night. Once Vanne wandered outside the tent in her sleep and collapsed. Dominic found her at three in the morning and helped her back to bed.

Goodall's fever broke first, and as soon as she felt better, she was anxious to continue her work. She was still plagued with worry that the study's funding would run out before she had accomplished anything significant. One morning while Vanne was still recovering in bed, her daughter set out alone, without her customary guide to accompany her. She still felt weak from her illness and had to stop several times to catch her breath. But she finally reached the top of a mountain peak about one thousand feet above the lake. From this perch she could view the entire Kakombe Stream Valley, where the chimpanzees fed, through her binoculars. She sat and waited.

After only fifteen minutes had passed, the movements of a group of chimps on a neighboring slope about eighty feet away caught her eye. Her position atop the peak put her in plain sight of them, but instead of running from her, they merely stared and then calmly moved on. Goodall stationed herself at her lookout post until evening. Several groups of chimps passed below her, stopping to feed on fig trees, then moving off in one large group to cross a stream, infants perched on their mothers' backs. It was the best day of observation she had had since her arrival.

The Peak

Discovering the Peak, which Goodall soon came to refer to with a capital letter, was the turning point in her work. It offered her an excellent vantage point to observe the chimps' behavior. It also allowed them to keep an eye on her and to realize that she would not try to follow them. Thus they were able to gradually get used to her strange presence in their world. And because the African guides always knew where she would be, they no longer needed to follow her, aside from checking on her in the evening to make sure she was still all right. At last Goodall could be alone with the chimpanzees.

The Peak quickly became Goodall's second campsite. She carried a small tin trunk up to the Peak that contained coffee and sugar, a kettle, a tin mug, a sweater, and a blanket. When she looked at the little trunk she may have been re-

The Peak

Jane Goodall's discovery of the Peak was the turning point in her research because it provided her with the ideal vantage point for observing the chimpanzees without frightening them off. This excerpt is from Walking with the Great Apes, *by Sy Montgomery.*

"Nearly every day she would make the predawn pilgrimage to the Peak. . . . No longer did the scouts need to accompany her; they knew Jane was safe up there. They knew where to reach her. Carrying her clothing and a thermos, she would often climb the mountain naked in the glimmering dawn. Though she carried her clothes so they would not become wet and cold in the dew, she came to enjoy the feel of the wet grass against her legs, the cool darkness wrapping her body. It was like a purification ritual before going to a sacred place. Though the spot is still used today by Gombe research workers, it is considered to belong in some way to her alone; they call it Jane's Peak.

At the Peak Jane always donned the same dull-colored clothing, and once seated, she remained utterly still. Clearly visible, with her presence Jane reiterated [repeated] her promise to the chimps, an incantation, an offering: I am here. I am harmless. I wait. To you, said her silent form, I give the choice: to flee or approach or ignore."

minded of the trunk containing cocoa and mugs that the Alligator Club members had used when they were girls. Although she always returned to camp to tell her mother about her day and write up her notes, Goodall sometimes went back to the Peak to sleep overnight if chimpanzees were sleeping in the area.

Every day for about a month, Goodall climbed the Peak, always wearing the same sort of neutral clothing so the chimps would get used to her appearance. There she pieced together her first impressions of chimpanzee life. She learned that the apes liked to move in small groups of about four to eight individuals. Sometimes one or two chimps would leave a group and wander off alone or join up with a different group. On other occasions two or three small groups would combine to form a large one.

Sociable Animals

She also learned that chimpanzees were not the violent, fearsome beasts others believed them to be. They were affectionate with each other, often greeting one another with hugs and kisses the way humans do. They also held hands like humans, and

Goodall witnessed chimp behavior firsthand and was able to disprove many of the stereotypes about it. In contrast to their reputation as vicious, Goodall found chimps playful and affectionate.

Goodall even saw one chimp extend a hand for another to kiss. The infants played rough-and-tumble games, and often two or more adults would spend long moments grooming one another, combing through the hair of their companions.

Their sleeping habits were also similar to humans', Goodall observed. Like people, chimpanzees sleep all night. From the Peak, Goodall watched as they prepared their nests in the evening. Each chimp made its own nest in the fork of a tree trunk or between two branches. They bent smaller branches over this foundation, holding each one in place with their feet and bending it back over the previous branch. Most of the chimps then made

themselves pillows of soft leafy twigs before settling in for the night. Baby chimps slept curled in their mothers' arms. Several times, if she could climb to reach a nest, Goodall would try it out after the chimpanzee who made it had left it behind at daybreak. She was impressed by the springy softness and careful weaving of the constructions.

Already, Goodall's vantage point at the Peak had allowed her to see similarities between chimpanzees and humans. She had learned something about the way they traveled, socialized, and slept. All these observations pointed to a gentler, more sociable creature than the common view of the ferocious chimpanzee depicted.

About one hundred chimpanzees lived at Gombe, and ultimately Goodall would observe about fifty of them. It was not long before she began to recognize individual chimpanzees. She gave them names based on their appearance or behavior. A strong, aggressive chimp became Goliath, and his friendly companion with a rim of white hair around his chin was David Greybeard. Goodall named one female chimp Olly because the animal reminded her of her Aunt Olly. Later Goodall learned that other scientists of her day disapproved of her naming the primates she studied. By naming her study subjects, they believed, she showed that she could not maintain the emotional detachment required of scientists. But thinking of the chimpanzees as individual personalities came naturally to Goodall and helped her perceive patterns in their reasoning and actions.

Two Amazing Discoveries

Goodall's patient, observational style was rewarded with breakthrough discoveries about chimps in the first few months of her research. These discoveries were significant because they challenged commonly held views. Her first important discovery was that chimpanzees eat meat. In the fifth month of her study, Goodall saw David Greybeard sitting in a tree with a female and a young chimpanzee, who both reached toward his mouth as if begging. David was chewing on a pink object that Goodall realized was meat. David shared his meal with the other chimps by spitting pieces of it into their hands. Once he dropped a chunk of meat for the young

chimp to retrieve. While the chimp was on the ground, an adult bushpig ran into the open and charged at it, accompanied by three piglets. Goodall then realized that the chimpanzees must be eating a piglet.

Because chimpanzees and their eating habits were so difficult to observe, scientists had previously assumed that chimpanzees were vegetarians. They believed that the apes sometimes ate insects or small rodents but had not known that chimpanzees could hunt other mammals. They had thought that only humans hunted and ate large mammals and shared the meat.

Her second important discovery occurred only two weeks later, on her way up to the Peak. Goodall spotted David Greybeard again in the grass about sixty yards away. She trained her binoculars on him. He was sitting next to a termite mound, similar to an anthill. He pushed a long grass stem into the mound, waited a few minutes. then withdrew the stem and popped it into his mouth. Goodall returned several times to the area of the termite mound. On the eighth day David reappeared with his friend Goliath. Each of them used stems they plucked themselves to dip into the termite mound. The insects would automatically cling to the foreign object. Then the chimps used the stem as a utensil to convey the tasty insects into their mouths. Goodall also noticed that the chimps would bite off the ends of their stems if they became bent or carefully peel the leaves from twigs to turn them into termite-fishing tools.

Goodall had watched chimpanzees make and use tools. Before this discovery scientists believed that only humans could use tools. In fact, the ability to use and make tools was part of the prevailing scientific definition of being human.

Redefining Humanity

Goodall was well aware of the importance of these two discoveries. In *My Friends the Wild Chimpanzees*, she writes:

At that time my mother had not yet left the reserve, and I was so excited I could hardly wait for sunset to hurry down and tell her what I had seen. . . .

"Can you really say that he was truly making tools?" my mother asked.

I described how David had stripped leaves from the section of vine and trimmed the edges off the blade of grass.

"He didn't just make use of any old bit of material lying around," I explained. "He actually modified stems and grasses and made them suitable for his purpose."

"Then that means man isn't the only toolmaker after all!" my mother exclaimed.[23]

Goodall cabled Louis Leakey immediately with her findings: humans were not the only primates to hunt mammals and share meat, nor were they the only primates to make and use tools. Leakey was

---

What Is Human?

One of Jane Goodall's most important discoveries was that chimpanzees can make and use tools. She describes the discovery's implications in My Friends the Wild Chimpanzees.

"Anthropologists, other social scientists, and theologians have defined man in a variety of ways. Until recently one widely accepted element of the anthropologists' definition was that 'man starts at that stage of primate evolution when the creature begins to make tools to a regular and set pattern.' The grasses and twigs used by the chimps for termite fishing do not, perhaps, comply entirely with this specification. Nonetheless, Dr. Leakey, on learning of my findings and referring to the description above, wrote, 'I feel that scientists holding to this definition are faced with three choices: They must accept chimpanzees as man, by definition; they must redefine man; or they must redefine tools.'

It is of great satisfaction to me to know that my work at the Gombe Stream Game Reserve is being taken into consideration by many scientists in their continuing efforts to redefine man in a manner far more complex and detailed than ever before attempted."

Chimpanzees use a stick tool to catch termites. Before Goodall witnessed this behavior, humans were thought to be the only species to use tools.

thrilled by her discoveries. According to Goodall in *My Friends the Wild Chimpanzees:* "Dr. Leakey, on learning of my findings . . . wrote, 'I feel that scientists holding to this definition are faced with three choices: They must accept chimpanzees as man, by definition; they must redefine man; or they must redefine tools.' "[24]

These early findings of Goodall's stirred up worldwide excitement. As writer Virginia Morell put it, "[Goodall's discoveries] blew apart anthropology's conception of primates—and human beings."[25] Morell's article quotes a primatologist at Princeton University, Alison Jolly, on her reaction in 1962 to Goodall's earthshaking news: "She essentially redefined what it is to be a human being. We'd all been brought up on 'man-the-tool-maker' and this just took it apart. Everyone knew that things would never be the same again."[26]

4 Acceptance

Louis Leakey wrote to the National Geographic Society about his young researcher's findings and their scientific importance. The U.S. branch of the society agreed to grant Goodall and Leakey funding for another year of research.

Each day Goodall reported news of the chimpanzees to her mother back at their campsite. Vanne was a sympathetic listener who praised each new discovery. But she was also a warm, outgoing woman who did not sit idle while her daughter was working. Instead, Vanne began to get to know the local residents and soon earned their respect.

The Medicine Woman

The women had arrived at Gombe with a first-aid kit filled with aspirin, ointments, bandages, and Epsom salts. When curious neighbors dropped by to get a good look at the strange white women, Vanne offered to try to treat any minor ailments they might have. One day a man with a hugely swollen leg hobbled into their camp with two deep sores on his lower leg. The festering sores had already begun to eat away at the bone. Vanne tried to persuade the man to go to the hospital, but

he refused. So she treated him herself with a home remedy called a saline drip. She instructed her patient to sit down twice a day with a large bowl of warm saltwater, which he was to drip slowly over his sores. After three weeks the swelling went down and the wounds were cleansed. Soon he was completely healed.

Word spread quickly. Soon Vanne was running a well-attended medical clinic every morning. She not only helped cure many medical problems but established good relations with their neighbors through her good deeds. Although most of the Africans found the women slightly crazy for abandoning civilization in favor of ape watching, they responded to Vanne's goodwill gestures with friendliness of their own.

Some of the villagers even began showing an interest in Goodall's work. One day Dominic told Goodall of an old man, Mbrisho, who had watched four chimpanzees chase away a lion with sticks. The story sounded far-fetched, but Goodall was willing to investigate. After a four-hour walk through the village of Bubango and up a mountainside to the old man's hut, she discovered that it was not Mbrisho himself who had seen the chimps drive off the lion, but one of his long-dead ancestors. However, she and the old man became friends, and he brought her a gift of eggs whenever he came to visit.

Thanks to Vanne, Goodall developed a friendly relationship with the local Africans. The animals posed more of a danger than the people. Gombe Stream Game Reserve was home to relatively little dangerous wildlife. Cobras were one notable exception. Goodall describes an early encounter with one of them:

> One evening when I was wading in the shallows of the lake to pass a rocky outcrop, I suddenly stopped dead as I saw the sinuous black body of a snake in the water. It was all of six feet long, and from the slight hood and the dark stripes at the back of the neck I knew it to be a Storm's water cobra—a deadly reptile for the bite of which there was, at that time, no serum. As I stared at it an incoming wave gently deposited part of its body on one of my feet. I remained motionless, not even breathing, until the wave rolled back into the lake, drawing the snake with it. Then I leaped out of the water as fast as I could, my heart hammering. . . . There is something utterly unnerving about a snake in the water.[27]

Vanne distributes aspirin to the local population. Goodall's mother offered to treat the villagers' minor ailments.

Walk Like a Chimpanzee

In her autobiography, My Life with the Chimpanzees, *Jane Goodall describes what it is like to keep up with chimpanzees in the wild.*

"It is not easy to follow chimps for a long time. . . . They go along their own pathways, moving easily through thick tangles of thorny undergrowth. To follow, you must crawl after them on all fours, or even wriggle along on your tummy, like a snake. Thorns catch at your clothes, your hair, and your skin. . . . As you struggle to pull free, you see the black shapes ahead vanishing, and you almost cry with frustration.

If you are lucky, you find the chimps again when you emerge from your battles with the vegetation. There they are, feeding peacefully in a tree, or resting quietly on the ground and grooming each other. Then you can relax and gather energy for the next journey.

The Tanzanian field staff are wonderful at following the chimps, even through the most difficult places, up the steepest and most treacherous slopes. But even they get defeated when the chimps cross a narrow, steep-sided valley by swinging from tree to tree, or when they climb a sheer cliff by shinnying up slender vines, or if they suddenly decide to travel really fast and silently.

However difficult it is to follow them, however much you get scratched and bruised, it's always worth it if you can keep up."

A chimp munches on a branch. Goodall's persistence with the chimps allowed her to view previously unheard-of behavior, such as using tools.

Four months after their arrival at Gombe together, Goodall's mother had to return home to England. Thanks to Vanne's clinics, Goodall was accepted by the local residents. The Kigoma authorities no longer worried about her living alone at Gombe. As Goodall put it: "I was by then part of the Gombe Stream landscape."[28] Goodall would have Hassan, a guide who had helped them at Lake Victoria, nearby to drive the boat and pick up supplies for her. But she would miss Vanne:

How lucky I was to have a mother like Vanne—a mother in a million. I could not have done without her during those early days. . . . She helped me to keep up my spirits during the depressing weeks when I could get nowhere near the chimps. How nice it was to come back in the evening and find a warm welcome. How pleasant to be able to discuss the events of the day, frustrating or exciting, over the fire during supper, and to hear the gossip of camp.[29]

Goodall did not fear solitude, however, and she had her fascinating primate companions to keep her busy. Wandering through the forest, she was able to gradually get closer to the chimps, especially to an old, weatherbeaten-looking female named Flo, who seemed to fear nothing. Flo was probably over thirty years old, her teeth worn down to the gums, her ears scarred and tattered, her nose bulbous. But she seemed to command the respect of the other chimps, even the males, who are socially dominant over the females. Flo was usually accompanied by a son, about four years old, whom Goodall named Figan, and a two-year-old infant named Fifi.

Goodall was able to get even closer to the chimpanzees during the rainy season, which had begun in October 1960, soon after Vanne had left. When the leaves strewn along the forest floor became damp from the rains, Goodall could silently approach some of the shyer chimps. Also, during wet weather chimpanzees tended to sit out in the open, hunched over, waiting out the storm. Mothers allowed their infants to huddle underneath them, so the young chimpanzees emerged completely dry after the shower.

A Strange Rain Dance

One day Goodall witnessed strange behavior on the part of some male chimpanzees at the beginning of a storm. As a clap of thunder shook the forest and the first raindrops began pelting down, a big male stood on his hind legs and swayed back and forth rhythmically, as if dancing. Then he charged off headlong down a slope. Two other males followed, dragging branches down the slope with them. One of them stopped short and shook a tree trunk back and forth until the branches shivered. Then they all ran back up the slope and down again, hooting fiercely while rain cascaded around them. The females and young chimps sat and watched from the trees during the dramatic performance. After about twenty minutes of ferocious charging up and down the slope, the males returned to the trees, the females and youngsters climbed down, and the whole group moved on. Goodall would only see such a performance, or "rain dance," twice more in the next ten years.

Goodall nears a group of chimps. Goodall braved the chimps' aggressive behavior until the aggression finally gave way to acceptance.

It was also during the rainy season that several of the male chimpanzees began getting closer to Goodall as she walked through the forest, approaching her in a threatening manner. Once Goliath, the large, aggressive male, shook branches at her from a treetop and screamed at her. Several other males joined in, surrounding her. Even when the end of a branch hit her on the head and Goliath's screams rose to a deafening pitch, Goodall stood her ground, looking away, and pretended to feed off leaves on the ground to show that she was not a threat. Suddenly the aggressive display stopped and the chimpanzees were gone.

About three weeks later Goodall was waiting near a tree that was heavy with ripe fruit, hoping chimpanzees would arrive to feed from it. When she heard a group of chimps approaching, she lay down under the plastic sheet that protected her from the drizzle, not wanting to scare the apes off. This time, instead of marching past her, a large male climbed a tree and screamed at her in a frenzy of rage, showering her with leaves and twigs. Then he climbed down the tree trunk and disappeared. Goodall kept still, listening to his footsteps approaching from behind. The ape made a loud barking sound, stamped his foot, and pounded her on the head. She sat up. The male chimp stared at her, then moved off. She felt as pleased as she had been frightened, because the chimpanzee had dared to make contact with her. She assumed he struck her because he was puzzled by her stillness and by her plastic covering. He had probably just wanted to goad her until she moved, she reasoned.

When Goodall told Dominic and Hassan about the incident, they spread the word. Her neighbors were impressed. An African had once climbed a palm tree filled with ripe fruit without noticing a male chimp feeding in the treetop. The chimp had lashed out at the man's face, putting out an eye. The news that Goodall had survived unharmed an encounter with an angry male chimp gave her increased status among the villagers.

The aggressive displays lasted about five months. Goodall interpreted this behavior as progress compared to the way the chimpanzees had run away from her whenever she had come too close during the early days of her study. After this period of hostility, as the rainy season finally ended, David Greybeard and Goliath sat only a few feet away from Goodall, so close that she could almost hear them breathing.

"Aloneness as a Way of Life"

Four months after their arrival in Gombe, Vanne had to return to England. In her book In the Shadow of Man *Jane Goodall describes adjusting to her newfound solitude.*

"My fire seemed lonely when Vanne had gone. . . . As the weeks passed, however, I accepted aloneness as a way of life and I was no longer lonely. I was utterly absorbed in the work, fascinated by the chimps, too busy in the evenings to brood. In fact, had I been alone for longer than a year I might have become a rather strange person, for inanimate objects began to develop their own identities: I found myself saying 'Good morning' to my little hut on the Peak, 'Hello' to the stream where I collected my water. And I became immensely aware of trees; just to feel the roughness of a gnarled trunk or the cold smoothness of young bark with my hand filled me with a strange knowledge of the roots under the ground and the pulsing sap within. I longed to be able to swing through the branches like the chimps, to sleep in the treetops lulled by the rustling of the leaves in the breeze. In particular, I loved to sit in a forest when it was raining, and to hear the pattering of the drops on the leaves and feel utterly enclosed in a dim twilight world of greens and browns and dampness."

Two weeks later a chimp she had named Mike sat with his back to her about fifteen feet away, calmly glancing at her from time to time over his shoulder. At last many of the apes had begun to accept her alien presence among them as unusual, but not frightening. One day Goodall was sitting near David Greybeard and held out a ripe red palm nut to him. He looked away, then looked back. Once again she held out her palm. He reached out and took her hand, then released it. The joy she felt at moments like this completely made up for the many months of despair she had patiently endured at the beginning of her study. Writer Joyce A. Senn reports Goodall's response to the David Greybeard incident:

> "At that moment I didn't need a scientist to explain what had happened," Jane later wrote in her notes. "David Greybeard had communicated with me. It was as if he had said, 'Everything is going to be okay.' And for those few seconds, the wall between human and

Goodall gives David a banana. David was one of the first chimps with whom Goodall had close contact.

Looking in a Chimpanzee's Eyes

In Through a Window *Jane Goodall explores her feelings about what kind of mind lurks beneath the chimpanzee gaze.*

"Often I have gazed into a chimpanzee's eyes and wondered what was going on behind them. I used to look into Flo's, she so old, so wise. What did she remember of her young days? David Greybeard had the most beautiful eyes of them all, large and lustrous, set wide apart. They somehow expressed his whole personality, his serene self-assurance, his inherent dignity—and, from time to time, his utter determination to get his way. For a long time I never liked to look a chimpanzee straight in the eye—I assumed that, as is the case with most primates, this would be interpreted as a threat or at least as a breach of good manners. Not so. As long as one looks with gentleness, without arrogance, a chimpanzee will understand, and may even return the look. And then—or such is my fantasy—it is as though the eyes are windows into the mind. Only the glass is opaque so that the mystery can never be fully revealed."

chimpanzee was broken down. It was a reward far beyond my greatest hopes."[30]

After the rains it was soon summer again. The National Geographic Society had been asking Louis Leakey whether they could send a photographer to Goodall's campsite to record her study for a magazine article. Goodall was hesitant about the idea of an outsider's coming to Gombe, fearing that an intruder might interfere with the trust she had worked so hard to forge between herself and the chimpanzees. She suggested to Leakey that he send her sister Judy to take the photographs for *National Geographic*. Judy was not a professional photographer, but she was blonde and slender like Goodall, so her similar appearance might not alarm the chimpanzees. Goodall also knew that Judy would not interfere with her work just to get a good photograph. *National Geographic* was not willing to take the risk, but Leakey pulled some strings and managed to convince a British newspaper called *Reveille* to take a gamble on an amateur photographer. The newspaper paid Judy's expenses in return for a series of interviews with Goodall when she returned to England.

By the time Judy arrived, the rainy season had returned. She spent hours in the rain sheltered under a plastic sheet, but the chimps hardly ever appeared. However, she was able to get some good pictures of her sister, the camp, and some of the local fishermen.

Back to School

Meanwhile, Louis Leakey had advised Goodall that she would need a college degree in order for her findings to be taken seriously by the academic establishment. Leakey was proud of Goodall but he had been criticized by his colleagues for hiring a researcher who lacked a college diploma. Instead, her résumé included a secretarial school credential and a stint as a waitress.

Leakey negotiated a deal with Cambridge University, where he had studied and later taught. The university agreed to allow Goodall to bypass its bachelor's degree requirement and begin working immediately toward her doctorate. After taking several semesters of course work at Cambridge, she would submit a final report of her Gombe chimpanzee research as her doctoral dissertation and receive her doctorate in ethology. This, Leakey felt, would make her discoveries the work of a legitimate scientist rather than an amateur.

Goodall was less than thrilled with the prospect of leaving Gombe for one semester each year to return to London and go back to school. She would be missing the opportunity to observe the chimps during that period. And she did not feel as strongly as Leakey did that she needed a doctorate. But she agreed to the plan.

In December 1961 Goodall's sister helped her pack up camp and store the equipment in Kigoma in preparation for returning to England for her first college semester. Leakey met the women in Nairobi. Leaving the apes, whom she had already come to know as individuals, was hard on Goodall. She never liked to leave a job unfinished. She would soon learn that her life and work among creatures hauntingly similar to ourselves had just begun.

Chapter

5 Establishing an Identity

The early 1960s was a time of growth for Goodall. Her relationships with her colleagues and with the primates she studied developed and deepened. Her career became a challenge that she met with strength, deepening her connections with those around her in the process.

Between 1962 and 1965 Goodall attended one semester a year at Cambridge University, during Gombe's rainy winter season. The months she logged during cold and dismal English winters at Cambridge proved helpful to her in the long run, but they were nevertheless quite a

Goodall attended Cambridge University part-time during the rainy seasons in Africa.

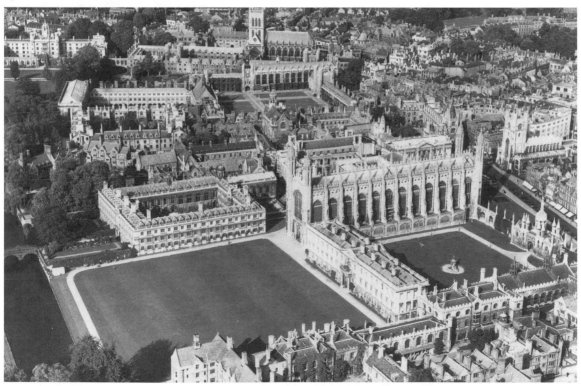

struggle for a student whose views on animals were quite different from those of her professors.

Ethologists Versus Naturalists

According to writer Sy Montgomery, in the late 1960s ethologists were trying to shake their reputations as naturalists and become recognized as scientists:

> Naturalists, typified by the self-taught nineteenth- and early twentieth-century explorers, merely scribbled descriptions in their notebooks. In the 1960s scientists . . . were supposed to be the saviors of the world. Guided by logic, propelled by measurement and experiment, scientists promised the breakthroughs leading to the Great Big Beautiful Tomorrow lauded at every World's Fair.[31]

The founder of ethology, Konrad Lorenz, an Austrian naturalist, relied on hours of observation without interference to make his famous discoveries, such as the phenomenon of imprinting, in which newly hatched ducklings will follow the first moving object they see as if it were their mother. He believed that animals had thoughts and emotions and behaved as they did for their own reasons. He did not experiment on or manipulate animals. He merely watched and interpreted their behavior.

But by the late 1950s Lorenz's passive approach to the study of animal behavior was no longer fashionable. The old school of naturalists were labeled butterfly collectors by the new breed of scientifically ori-

Naturalist Konrad Lorenz pioneered the technique of carefully observing animal behavior that Goodall imitated and improved upon. One of his discoveries was imprinting—the idea that newborn animals bond with whatever they see first.

ented researchers. The new ethologists saw animals as numbers, as problems to be solved, and they were fond of conducting experiments on their subjects. By the 1960s ethologists at Cambridge did not want to hear about individual animals. They wanted to discover the mechanics of behavior and saw the animals they studied as mere cogs and wheels in that universal machinery.

Goodall's Point of View

Goodall's view of ethology was decidedly different from that of her teachers. In her book, *Through a Window*, Goodall contrasts her ideas with the way it was fashionable to study and discuss animals in the 1960s:

> When I began my study at Gombe in 1960 it was not permissible—at least not in ethological circles—to talk about an animal's mind. Only humans had minds. Nor was it quite proper to talk about animal personality. Of course everyone knew that they *did* have their own unique characters—everyone who had ever owned a dog or other pet was aware of that. But ethologists, striving to make theirs a "hard" science, shied away from the task of trying to explain such things objectively.[32]

Goodall felt that her advisers adopted an impersonal stance toward the animals they studied in order to be taken seriously as scientists. She, on the other hand, had no deep-rooted desire to be seen as a scientist. She was simply interested in the chimpanzees.

Goodall took the approach of the traditional naturalist. In her first eighteen months at Gombe she had accumulated 850 typed pages of observations about the chimpanzees. The notes were in the form of narratives, or stories. Individual chimps, such as Flo and her daughter Fifi, or David Greybeard and his friend Goliath, were the main characters in her stories. As writer Virginia Morell puts it, "Goodall watched as life histories unfolded, believing that these lives—rather than theories or experiments—held the key to social structure."[33]

Goodall's emphasis on the individual life story was frowned on by other ethologists, most of whom were male at that time. According to Morell, "primatology was a bastion [stronghold] of male domination—and Goodall came under attack. The leading lights of the field considered [her] tendency [toward emphasizing individual life stories] unscientific and sentimental."[34]

Because Goodall was a female in a male-dominated field and her views differed from those of her male colleagues, her point of view was often described as a feminine one, according to writer Sy Montgomery: "Jane's approach was maverick for the very reason it was rejected: she was applying a feminine approach to a field that was dominated and defined by male views and values."[35]

Looking back several years later in *Through a Window*, Goodall writes that her approach was not so much feminine as simply logical:

> If we test the effect of drugs on chimpanzees because they arc biologically so similar to ourselves, if we accept that there are dramatic similarities in chimpanzee and human brain and nervous system, is it not logical to assume that there will be similarities also in at least the more basic feelings, emotions, moods of the two species?[36]

If scientists can admit that chimps and people are physically alike, why not admit that they are emotionally and mentally alike as well? Goodall asks.

Many of Goodall's colleagues at the time felt that focusing on emotions and personalities put the ethologist in danger of becoming too wrapped up in the subject matter. If a scientist becomes emotionally involved, it hurts the ability to make rational judgments, they maintained. In *Through a Window*, Goodall addressed this concern:

> Empathy and intuition can be of tremendous value as we attempt to understand certain complex behavioural interactions, provided that the behaviour, as it occurs, is recorded precisely and objectively. Fortunately I have seldom found it difficult to record facts in an orderly manner even during times of powerful emotional involvement.[37]

Not only her teachers, but also the scientific journals of the day, objected to Goodall's personal approach. As a student Goodall submitted an article for publication to a scientific journal, *Annals of the New York Academy of Science*. The journal sent her paper back to her. They wanted to publish it but insisted that she number the chimps instead of naming them, call

---

Not Things but Beings

When Jane Goodall began reporting her research while a student at Cambridge University, she discovered that ethologists of the day did not approve of discussing animals' personalities or emotions. Such things were reserved for humans. Goodall disagreed, as she writes in Through a Window.

"When I began my study at Gombe in 1960 it was not permissible—at least not in ethological circles—to talk about an animal's mind. Only humans had minds. Nor was it quite proper to talk about animal personality. Of course everyone knew that they *did* have their own unique characters—everyone who had ever owned a dog or other pet was aware of that. But ethologists, striving to make theirs a 'hard' science, shied away from the task of trying to explain such things objectively. . . .

How naive I was. . . . I didn't realize that animals were not supposed to have personalities, or to think, or to feel emotions or pain. I had no idea that it would have been more appropriate to assign each of the chimpanzees a number rather than a name when I got to know him or her. I didn't realize that it was not scientific to discuss behaviour in terms of motivation or purpose. And no one had told me that terms such as *childhood* and *adolescence* were uniquely human phases of the life cycle, culturally determined, not to be used when referring to young chimpanzees. Not knowing, I freely made use of all those forbidden terms and concepts in my initial attempt to describe, to the best of my ability, the amazing things I had observed at Gombe."

Goodall talks with Dr. Melvin Payne, executive vice president of the National Geographic Society, at a speaking engagement in Washington.

them "it" rather than "he" or "she," and use "which" rather than "who." Goodall refused to make the changes. The paper was published as she had written it.

Bruised Egos

The speed of Goodall's rise to success made her an object of jealousy to some of her associates at Cambridge. The fame she had achieved through her early discoveries, such as her discovery that chimps used and made tools, led to some bruised egos. According to Virginia Morell, "Goodall met with hostility from other researchers."[38] Many of them were jealous of the recogni-

tion she gained through articles in popular magazines such as *National Geographic*. Many male scientists made unkind personal remarks about Goodall, some even going so far as to call her a dumb blonde. They joked about her first name—"Me Jane, you Tarzan." Some ethologists even accused Goodall of making up her reports of chimps eating meat. Others hinted that she had taught the chimps to use tools herself. Some female colleagues made equally ugly comments. According to Sy Montgomery, one woman professor was overheard saying that the only reason Jane Goodall was so famous was "because of her great legs in those short shorts in the films."[39]

Ultimately, being at odds with the academic establishment worked to Goodall's advantage. She gained confidence from confronting disbelief and disapproval when she encountered them during her speaking engagements. She also learned to remain true to her own views, as she had when the scientific journal asked her to change the wording of her paper. She told Sy Montgomery in an interview, referring to Cambridge's academic establishment:

> I didn't give two hoots for what they thought. They were wrong, and I was right. That's why I was lucky that I never was going into any of these things for science. And as I didn't care about the Ph.D., it didn't matter. I would listen, I just wouldn't do what they said. Then I would go back to what I was doing at Gombe.[40]

Despite her stubbornness Goodall learned a great deal about how to put her ideas into a format that more traditional scientists could stomach. Her adviser, Robert Hinde, was sympathetic to her message, even though he was a little dismayed by her methods. In *Through a Window* Goodall recalls his help with gratitude:

> Robert gave me wonderful advice on how best to tie up some of my more rebellious ideas with scientific ribbon. "You can't *know* that Fifi was jealous," he admonished on one occasion. We argued a little. And then: "Why don't you just say *If Fifi were a human child we would say she was jealous.*" I did.[41]

Despite her differences with the academics at Cambridge, Jane Goodall made it through with distinction. After being featured several times in *National Geographic* and receiving the National Geographic Society's Franklin Burr Award for Contribution to Science in 1963 and 1964, Goodall earned her doctorate from Cambridge University in 1965. She could devote herself to her research and no longer concern herself with university politics.

6 Gombe Blossoms

The 1960s was also a time of new personal relationships for Jane Goodall. The presence of a husband, then a son, complicated her experience at Gombe and enriched her life in ways that had a positive influence on her work.

Hugo van Lawick Joins Goodall at Gombe

In 1962, when Goodall was twenty-eight, she met a man she felt was her counterpart in his love for animals and his commitment to his work. Hugo van Lawick was a Dutch baron who was born in Indonesia and educated in England and the Netherlands. He came to Gombe Stream Game Reserve in 1962. He was a photographer who had been working in East Africa, filming a popular television program called *On Safari.*

In Africa van Lawick met Louis and Mary Leakey and began work on a documentary for the National Geographic Society on the Leakeys' work at Olduvai Gorge. Leakey was impressed both by van Lawick's talent and his love of animals. He recommended the baron to *National Geographic* as the perfect person to document

Goodall's work at Gombe, a sensitive job that Goodall's sister had attempted with only partial success the year before. Simultaneously, Leakey wrote to Goodall's mother to inform her that he had found the perfect husband for Goodall.

Around the time of van Lawick's arrival, after Goodall had returned from her first semester at Cambridge, another breakthrough in Goodall's Gombe research occurred. Some of the chimpanzees had become bold enough to venture into Goodall's camp. At first only David would wander into the area and feed from the palm tree that shaded her tent. After the palm tree's fruit was gone, Goodall instructed Dominic to leave bananas out to attract the chimps. At unpredictable times David, first alone, then later followed by Goliath and then William, would wander into the campsite and look for bananas.

On van Lawick's first morning at Gombe, he hid himself and his camera behind a tent flap while David helped himself to bananas, not wanting to startle the chimp. But after he finished eating, the ape ambled over, pulled back one of the flaps, stared at van Lawick, then grunted and shuffled away. The other two chimpanzees accepted van Lawick with an equal lack of surprise.

Photographer Hugo van Lawick worked with Goodall, documenting on film her work with chimpanzees. The two would later marry.

Caught on Film

Thus, on van Lawick's first day he got great shots on film of the three males greeting one another, grooming, and begging each other for bananas. Next Goodall took him up to the Peak. Van Lawick was able to film two young male chimpanzees hunting, killing, and eating a monkey. Goodall had only seen chimps eating meat one other time since she had seen David Greybeard sharing the carcass of a baby pig with the others. That time she had seen chimpanzees eating a young bushbuck, but she could not be certain that they had actually killed the bushbuck themselves. On the Peak Goodall and van Lawick witnessed the chimps grab a red colobus monkey and tear it to pieces. Van Lawick did not have time to film the hunt but was able to document the chimpanzees eating their kill.

It took the chimpanzees a little while to accept van Lawick's presence among them in the forest, but gradually they got used to his loud cameras. Van Lawick was careful not to make sudden movements. His visit was soon interrupted by the arrival of the yearly rains, but in his last ten days, he was able to film David, William, and Goliath demonstrating their toolmaking and tool using at the termite hill. According to Goodall, "It was exciting material, and Hugo hoped that it would help him to persuade the Geographic Society to let him return the following year and continue filming the chimpanzees."[42]

Wordless Speech

In her first book, My Friends the Wild Chimpanzees, *Jane Goodall analyzes the ways chimpanzees communicate without words.*

"The apes have a large vocabulary of calls, each signifying an emotion such as fear, pain, or pleasure. When a group arrives at a food-laden tree and gives excited 'food barks,' other chimps within earshot often call in response and hurry to the feast. If one chimp gives a low, uneasy 'hoo' when he sights an alarming object, others always peer in the same direction. When a youngster screams in fright or pain his mother invariably hurries to him.

The chimpanzees have also evolved a complex nonverbal communication based on touch, posture, and gesture, in many respects almost identical to the nonverbal communication used by man. Gesture and facial expression play a major part among humans. For instance, an arm placed gently around another's shoulder may convey a message of sympathy more eloquently than words. . . .

Chimpanzees rely to a very great extent on communication by touch during their interactions. Physical contact seems to play a particularly vital role in the apes' emotional life, especially during infancy, when the mother's touch provides the youngster with its chief source of security. . . .

Chimpanzees, like people, exchange greetings when they meet. . . . When this occurs, an observer can usually determine the relationship of one chimp to the other. They may meet as two friends and show pleasure in their reunion, or one may make submissive gestures, acknowledging the other's higher rank. . . .

Many of the apes' forms of greeting startlingly resemble our own. They often kiss. . . . Hand-holding, as a gesture of greeting, is not common . . . but it does occur. . . .

The similarity of many chimpanzee gestures and postures to those of man is to Hugo and me one of the most exciting aspects of our study."

Goodall's Soul Mate

After van Lawick left Gombe, Goodall was alone again. But her solitude was not as satisfying as it had been before his arrival. Van Lawick had impressed her with his willingness to share in her work. She felt that she may have found a soul mate in him:

> I had found in Hugo a companion with whom I could share not only the joys and frustrations of my work but also my love of the chimpanzees, of the forests and mountains, of life in the wilderness. He had been with me into some of the wild, secret places where, I thought, no other white person would ever tread. . . . In Hugo I knew I had found a kindred spirit—one who had a deep appreciation and understanding of animals. Small wonder that I missed him when he was gone.[43]

In 1962 Goodall returned to London for another Cambridge semester, returning to Gombe the following spring. Her *National Geographic* articles had aroused public interest in chimpanzees. And so the following summer the magazine sent Hugo van Lawick back to Gombe to take more photographs. Again they parted, but this time van Lawick sent Goodall a telegram the next day asking her to marry him. It was just before Christmas 1963. She accepted his proposal.

They married in London, after Goodall completed her next semester at Cambridge, on March 28, 1964. Instead of putting a miniature bride and groom on

Van Lawick proposed to Goodall via telegram. They married in London in 1964.

Flo with her son Flint. Goodall claimed she learned how to be a good mother by watching Flo.

their wedding cake, the couple topped the cake with a clay chimpanzee. The reception hall walls sported enlargements of Hugo's photographs of the Gombe chimpanzees—Flo and her children, Fifi, Faben, and Figan; David Greybeard; and Goliath.

The couple seemed to share a single focus. The object of that focus was the Gombe chimps, as the newlyweds made clear by trimming their honeymoon to three days so they could return to Africa in time for the birth of Flo's baby, the first chimp Goodall would be able to observe from earliest infancy. The newlyweds were keenly interested in what kind of mother Flo would turn out to be to her new son, Flint. They would remember what they had observed when Goodall gave birth to their own son three years later. According to Sy Montgomery, Goodall learned from

Studying the Hyena

Jane Goodall and her husband Hugo studied other animals as well as chimps. In this passage from My Life, *she discovers that hyenas and chimps have much in common.*

"When Grub was a tiny baby, Hugo and I were studying hyenas in Ngorongoro Crater. You probably think of hyenas as skulking, cowardly scavengers, waiting for scraps left by the lions. Don't believe it! They are great hunters, going after [wildebeests] and zebras, as well as smaller creatures. . . .

Hyenas are actually very interesting creatures. Like chimps, they wander around in little groups of friendly individuals. Like chimps, they have very distinct personalities and fascinating behavior. Like chimps, they are territorial and may kill hyenas from neighboring clans. . . .

I loved studying those Ngorongoro hyenas. At night, when there was a moon, I would drive our VW camper to a hyena den where there were one or two tiny black cubs. Grub was usually asleep in the back of the car. As dusk settled, other, older cubs would begin to appear. They were coming to play with the little ones, the ones who were not old enough to go visiting.

What wonderful games went on around those dens in the moonlight! Sometimes the cubs played tag with an ostrich feather or an old bone. They had mock battles and tumbled over and over, wrestling and biting."

Flo about motherhood almost as if Flo herself were a mother figure, and Goodall's later personal experience of motherhood allowed her to understand Flo better:

In Flo, Jane found the wizened old wise-woman; Jane was her initiate. To Jane, as to no other human, Flo would pass on her experience of sexuality, of motherhood, of the wisdom that comes with maturity. . . . Jane learned from Flo, a chimpanzee, how to be a human mother. And in turn, Jane's own unfolding life deepened her understanding of Flo's life.[44]

An Affectionate Mother

The couple often witnessed the old mother chimpanzee, Flo, perform a playful act with her baby son. She would lie on her back and dangle her baby above her, holding him by the wrist with her foot. With one of her hands she would reach up and tickle him while he smiled, wiggled, and kicked in delight. Flo's five-year-old daughter, Fifi, would look on in fascination, reaching out to touch the baby with her fingertips. Soon Fifi would be allowed to cuddle and tickle the infant herself. Goodall was to observe many other mother-child relationships among the Gombe chimpanzees. Not all were as affectionate and relaxed as the relationships between Flo and her children. Goodall would realize that mothering styles among the chimps varied, just as they varied among human mothers and children.

Goodall found Flo a model mother. She admired Flo's ability to shower her children with affection. Flo continually groomed them and caressed them, and if she had to discipline them mildly, she would reassure them with a hug afterward. She rushed to their sides if they whimpered or called to her. If they looked like they were about to get into trouble, she would distract them with tickling.

The New Baby

When Goodall became pregnant, Flo's maternal behavior became doubly interesting. Goodall and van Lawick decided to apply many of Flo's parenting techniques to the raising of their own child, Hugo Eric Louis, whom they nicknamed Grub. The couple brought Grub to Gombe when he was four months old. Like little Flint, Grub was cradled and carried almost constantly, and he was breast-fed on demand in a decade when most women bottle-fed their babies. But unlike little Flint, Grub faced dangers that a chimpanzee baby did not need to be protected from. Goodall and her husband had to figure out a way to keep their beloved son safe from the wild chimpanzees.

The couple had heard reports about two separate incidents in the 1940s of chimpanzees carrying off human infants and eating them. So Goodall and van Lawick built a huge playpen for their baby, a sort of cage of wire mesh painted light blue, with models of birds and stars hanging gaily from its ceiling. The enclosure, containing the baby's crib, was placed inside the little one-room cottage the couple shared. Thus, even if chimpanzees broke into the cottage, Grub would be safe inside the cage. Later, when little Grub could walk, his parents built a caged-in patio for him to play in. Whenever he played outside, one of his parents or another adult was with him. Grub quickly learned to crawl, walk, and swim. He often ran around naked, exploring the streams, forests, and beach with his parents.

Many of the couple's friends were rather shocked by the way the couple were raising their son. They thought that living among chimpanzees would harm the child's development and they disapproved of the way Grub's parents comforted him every time he cried. In those days it was fashionable to allow a child to cry alone occasionally, since it was thought this would help children become independent. When Grub began running naked around Gombe, some observers were worried that he would become a wild boy.

While Grub was allowed to run as free as any chimp he still remembers being afraid of the chimpanzees, who gave him threatening looks and often teased him. Once van Lawick was walking through the forest with Grub on his shoulders, and Flo's baby, Flint, suddenly reached out from behind a tree and pulled Grub's hair. Writer Ron Arias quotes Grub on his uneasy relationship with the apes as a child:

> "If you raise your eyebrows and stare at them, it's like a threat," Grub once explained. "Of course, if you're safe in a cage it's quite fun—they will come and bang on it. But they remember you, and when they see you outside, they will come for you."[45]

Goodall adjusted her work schedule to be with Grub. When he was three years old, she and van Lawick hired two African nannies to watch him in the mornings. While he played on the beach, Goodall went to her office to write, type research notes, or work on funding grant applications. Van Lawick worked on his photography. Goodall spent every afternoon with her son. When he got older, the couple hired a tutor, who gave him regular lessons every morning. Grub was also free to play with the African children his age and quickly learned to speak KiSwahili and KiHa as well as English.

Stay-at-Home Mothers

Flo's influence on Goodall's parenting philosophy became a central message in her many lectures in the United States and England, according to Sy Montgomery. In front of members of the National Geographic Society, for example, Goodall might point to a behavior of Flo's that was captured on film as a positive example of mothering. Goodall placed a lot of importance on the mother-child rela-

tionship and in her lectures often applauded stay-at-home mothers. Her comments met with mixed response:

> Some of Jane's comments made her unpopular with feminists, who saw her as reinforcing the stereotypical female role just as they were succeeding in enlarging women's horizons. But Goodall best remembers the comments of young mothers who would come up to her after her talks. "Thank you," she remembers one young woman saying, "for giving me the courage to spend time with my children."[46]

Goodall with her son, Hugo, affectionately called Grub. Van Lawick and Goodall believed in rearing Grub similarly to the way chimpanzees reared their young.

Bringing Up Baby

In her book In the Shadow of Man, *Jane Goodall discusses how she and her first husband took their cues from chimpanzee mothers when raising their own infant son.*

"I was at the Gombe Stream for several months during 1966 when my own child was on the way and also during the following year when he was with me as a tiny baby. I watched the chimpanzee mothers coping with their infants with a new perspective. From the start Hugo and I had been impressed with many of their techniques, and we made a deliberate resolve to apply some of these to the raising of our own child. First, we determined to give our baby a great deal of physical contact, affection, and play. He was breast-fed, more or less on demand, for a year. He was not left to scream in his crib. Wherever we went we took him with us so that though his environment was often changing, his relationship with his parents remained stable. When we punished him we quickly gave him reassurance through physical contact and, when he was small, we tried to distract him rather than simply prevent him from doing something naughty. . . .

Has our method of bringing him up been successful? We cannot say as yet. We can only point out that today, at four years of age, he is obedient, extremely alert and lively, mixes well with other children and adults alike, is relatively fearless and is thoughtful of others. In addition, and quite contrary to the predictions of many of our friends, he is very independent. But then, of course, he might have been like this anyway, even if we had brought him up in a quite different way."

The Growth of the Research Center

The solitary adventure Goodall had begun at Gombe had expanded to include others—first Hugo van Lawick, then volunteers who wrote and asked if they could be a part of Goodall's research. In 1964 Gombe's first research assistant, a young woman volunteer, arrived from Peru. Another soon followed in 1965. These two women helped enormously with the mounting load of paperwork generated by Goodall's detailed field notes. But the work was still more than the three women and van Lawick could manage.

The National Geographic Society remained an enthusiastic sponsor of Goodall's work. It responded to her requests for additional funding, allowing her to hire students from Cambridge and Stanford, in California, as well as from the university at Dar es Salaam, Tanzania's capital. Goodall recalls in *Through a Window:*

> There were graduate students from a variety of disciplines, mainly anthropology, ethology and psychology, from universities in the United States and Europe. And there were undergraduates too, from the interdisciplinary human biology programme at Stanford University and from the zoology department of the university of Dar es Salaam.[47]

To give her a place to put all the people and data, the National Geographic Society also contributed the money to erect simple housing and office buildings at Gombe. A mess hall was set up in a cement building by the beach, which also contained offices and a generator for electricity. Another small stone room housed van Lawick's photography darkroom. The students slept in prefabricated aluminum huts tucked away in the trees near the camp.

According to Goodall, "the Gombe Stream Research Centre grew from small beginnings to become one of the most dynamic field stations for the study of animal behaviour in the world."[48] Its ties were international. According to Bettyann Kevles:

> The Tanzanian government incorporated the old chimpanzee reserve into its larger national park system in 1968. At almost the same time, Dr. Goodall was appointed director of the scientific field station that had been renamed the Gombe Stream Research Center. The Center began to develop ties with universities on three continents: to Cambridge in England, where Goodall had received her Ph.D. in 1965; Stanford in California, where she was a visiting professor from 1971 to 1975; and the university at Dar es Salaam, on the other side of Tanzania.[49]

The Students

Goodall, her family, and her students formed a close-knit community. At times graduate-school students are competitive when it comes to research; Goodall recalls with pleasure in *Through a Window* that this did not seem to be the case at her research center, perhaps because the students, like her, had fallen under what she terms "the spell of Gombe":

> There was a spirit of cooperation among the students, a willingness to share data, that was, I think, quite unusual. It had not been easy to foster this generous attitude—initially many of the graduate students were, understandably, reluctant to contribute any of their precious data to a central information pool. But clearly this had to be done."[50]

By 1975 the research center employed eight graduate students, ten undergraduates, and ten permanent Tanzanian animal observers. The students worked a twelve-hour day that coincided with the nest-to-nest cycle (from waking to sleeping) of the chimpanzees they tracked.

Despite the growing reputation of Goodall's center and work, she could not escape criticism of her methods. Increasingly the human element at Gombe began overlapping with the natural environment, introducing new stimuli for the chimps, but also threatening to artificially change their environment.

Mike's Rise to Power

The intermixing of human and ape environments became an issue for Goodall's critics on several occasions. Adult male chimps arrange themselves in a hierarchy, or rigid order, from the top-ranking male down to the lowest-ranking male. The top,

or alpha, male receives the deference of all the other chimpanzees, male and female. In 1963 Mike, a small adult chimp, was at the bottom of the hierarchy. By 1964, however, his standing had definitely changed. Mike would soon supplant Goliath in the position of alpha male chimpanzee.

When adult males wish to impress each other with their power, they engage in a behavior Goodall calls a charging display. Usually they seize a handful of twigs or small branches to shake threateningly as they rush forward, hooting loudly. Mike's approach was more creative. Empty four-gallon kerosene cans often accumulated at the research camp, and Mike decided to

Mike with the kerosene cans he would use to challenge male chimps who were higher in the hierarchy. Tolerance for such behavior led researchers to criticize Goodall's methods.

make use of them. He would pick up two cans by their handles, then charge toward the other higher-ranking males, banging the cans on the ground ahead of him with a horrible clatter and rattle that unnerved the males into rushing out of his way.

According to Goodall's *In the Shadow of Man*, Mike's use of man-made objects during his charging displays indicated his intelligence and ability to plan: "Charging displays usually occur at a time of emotional excitement. . . . But it seemed that Mike actually *planned* his charging displays; almost, one might say, in cold blood."[51]

Goodall speculates that Mike would have risen to the top without the aid of the kerosene cans:

Would Mike have become the top-ranking male if my kerosene cans and I had not invaded the Gombe Stream? We shall never know, but I suspect he would have in the end. Mike has a strong "desire" for dominance, a char-

---

Mike of the Terrible Cans

Goodall learned that chimpanzee social groups contain one dominant, or alpha, male. This male is usually the biggest or strongest, since he must impress all the other males with his power. But as she relates in her book In the Shadow of Man, *Goodall witnessed a chimp that was neither big nor strong rise to power by using his intellect—and an unusual prop. He kept his superior position for several years.*

"All at once Mike calmly walked over to our tent and took hold of an empty kerosene can by the handle. Then he picked up a second can and, walking upright, returned to the place where he had been sitting. Armed with his two cans Mike continued to stare toward the other males. . . . Suddenly he was off, charging toward the group of males, hitting the two cans [together] ahead of him. The cans, together with Mike's crescendo of hitting, made the most appalling racket: no wonder the . . . males rushed out of the way. . . .

Mike's deliberate use of man-made objects was probably an indication of superior intelligence. Many of the adult males had at some time or another dragged a kerosene can to enhance their charging displays in place of the more normal branches or rocks; but only Mike apparently had been able to profit from the chance experience and learn to seek out the cans deliberately to his own advantage. The cans, of course, made several times more noise than a branch when dragged along the ground at speed, and eventually Mike was able to keep three cans ahead of him at once for about sixty yards as he ran flat-out across the camp clearing. No wonder that males previously his superiors rushed out of Mike's way."

Flo holds onto son Flint's waist while Goodall extends the back of her hand to Flint.

acteristic very marked in some individuals and almost entirely lacking in others. Over and above this trait Mike has unquestionable intelligence—and amazing courage too.[52]

Perhaps Goodall's presence had interfered with chimpanzee life at Gombe. Goliath might have remained superior and Mike inferior if there had been no kerosene cans. Whether the researchers, accidentally or on purpose, meddled with the natural course of chimpanzee life at Gombe is a question that Goodall's critics often raise. They are disturbed most by Goodall's decisions during a critical period when the chimpanzees began visiting the camp on a regular basis.

The chimpanzees, gradually losing their fear of the strange human visitors, were lured by the sweet new fruit, the banana, that was not naturally available to them at Gombe. Flo, the fearless old female, was fond of bananas and often visited

Close Contact

When Jane Goodall and Hugo van Lawick first began working with the chimpanzees that entered the camp, they delighted in roughhousing with the little ones. In In the Shadow of Man, *Goodall explains why she later came to feel that this was a mistake.*

"Not until Hugo and I had actually left the Gombe Stream did we realize that during the year we had made one grave mistake. We had encouraged Flint to touch us and we had tickled him gently. It had been a delightful experience, and Flint had become more and more trusting. We had marveled that a wild chimpanzee mother could lose her fear of humans to the extent of allowing her infant to play with us. But Fifi had copied Flint's example, and so had Figan. At the time it had not seemed to matter; it proved . . . that it is possible to establish a close and friendly relation with a creature who has lived the first years of his life in fear of man. . . .

When we left we realized the foolishness of our behavior. The adult male chimpanzee is at least three times stronger than a man; if Figan grew up and realized how much weaker humans really were, he would become dangerous. Moreover, repeated contact with a wild animal is bound to affect its behavior. We made a rule that in the future no student should purposefully make contact with any of the chimpanzees."

camp to feed on them. She brought her family with her, including her young son Figan. According to Kevles:

> Goodall began wrestling with Figan and tickling him. But when she realized that she had stepped over the line from habituating them [getting them used to people] into taming them, she stopped. She was also endangering both herself and other future human observers. Adult chimpanzees are much stronger than humans. And while the infants enjoyed playing . . . the same animal, full grown, could

initiate the same games and accidentally squeeze the life out of its human playmate.[53]

While she acknowledged her error in judgment in petting the chimpanzees who came to camp, Goodall continued supplying the chimps with bananas. She and van Lawick set up what they called a feeding station, a series of boxes rigged to supply chimps with bananas on a controlled basis. According to Kevles:

> [Goodall] liked the idea of a "feeding station." It was an excellent way to get

to know the individuals and to watch them as they interacted in a group. . . . Goodall believes she got to know the wild animals better in a shorter span of time by feeding them bananas than she ever could have done by observing them among the trees.[54]

Even Louis Leakey, one of Goodall's strongest supporters, felt that Goodall had gone too far. He worried that the chimps would become too bold, lose their fear of humans and begin to raid villagers' houses. He feared that the animals would then be shot. According to Sy Montgomery, "Jane's provisioning the chimps with bananas was later strongly criticized, even by Louis, who vehemently objected."[55]

Goodall's other colleagues also questioned the practice, Kevles writes: "Some primate ethologists question the whole banana-feeding scheme. They argue that in giving the chimpanzees a food that they could not naturally find at Gombe, Goodall intervened with their 'natural' environment."[56] Goodall's goal was to observe, not to interfere. Introducing the bananas into the Gombe chimpanzees' environment might have made them behave in ways that were not natural to them, thus tainting the purity of the research.

However, Goodall saw the feeding of the chimpanzees as a stepping stone that allowed her to become a more intimate observer of the chimpanzees. Her offerings allowed Goodall and the chimpanzees to become closer to each other.

Chapter

7 Tragedy in Paradise

The 1970s was a tough decade for Goodall. She faced disillusionment in both her personal and professional life. During this period she and van Lawick divorced. In addition, Goodall learned something about her beloved chimpanzees that she would rather not have known: their capacity for violence was equal to that of humans. Also during this chaotic decade, the Gombe Stream Research Center became a pawn in interstate conflict, leading to the kidnapping of four of the center's researchers. With each shock Goodall stood firm, reaching out to the natural world for balance and for solace.

Divorce

When she married van Lawick, Goodall thought she had found her male counterpart, someone who felt and thought the way she did about the research work she was accomplishing at Gombe. But in assuming that van Lawick would always share her feelings, perhaps Goodall assumed too much. She and van Lawick were actually very different.

In *Walking with the Great Apes*, Goodall's former student Emilie Bergman recalls that van Lawick was a tense person, a

Goodall and van Lawick divorced in 1974. Goodall regretted the divorce, especially for its effect on their son, Grub.

chain-smoker who always seemed under pressure. He and Goodall once made an agreement to take one evening off a week to simply relax and enjoy each other's company. Otherwise, they both would have been working twenty-four hours a day. But increasingly they were interested in working on different things.

According to Bergman, quoted by Sy Montgomery, van Lawick was losing patience with putting his photography career on hold just to help Goodall run her research center. He began to complain that he was tired of being "Mr. Goodall." Tension mounted between them. A friend of the couple quoted in an article by writer Ron Arias recalls that "the differences in their backgrounds were exacerbated [increased] . . . by working together 24 hours a day and sharing the same tent year after year, with no communication with other people."[57]

In 1974 Baron Hugo van Lawick and Jane Goodall separated, then divorced. Their only child, Grub, was seven years old. In *My Life with the Chimpanzees* Goodall looks back on the painful event, wondering if she could somehow have saved the marriage or saved her son the pain the divorce caused him:

> Hugo's work, photographing and filming, took him all over the place. And I felt that it was important for me to spend most of my time at Gombe. We

stayed good friends, but it was sad, especially for Grub. If I could live that part of my life over again, I would try very hard to work things out differently.[58]

Derek Bryceson

Goodall put her pain behind her and carried on with her work. About a year after her divorce, she remarried. Her easygoing new husband, Derek Bryceson, known by her students as Mr. B., was the only white cabinet member in Tanzania's government. His job was to direct the country's national park system. He was also a close friend of Julius Nyerere, Tanzania's first president since gaining its independence in 1961. After their marriage Bryceson shared his beautiful home near the Indian Ocean in Dar es Salaam, Tanzania's capital, with Goodall and her son. When Goodall was working at Gombe, he visited her often, and they talked daily over a radio transmitter.

Goodall watches an African baboon the year of her divorce. She remarried within a year.

Bryceson had been a fighter pilot in World War II. He was permanently injured at the age of nineteen when his plane was shot down over the Middle East. The accident left him almost completely paralyzed from the waist down. Nevertheless, he was still able to get around by using only a cane, and he continued to fly an airplane with the help of another pilot to operate the foot controls during takeoffs and landings. Goodall admired his courage and willpower.

Bryceson often took his stepson fishing in Dar es Salaam. But when Grub was nine, he went to live with Goodall's mother in England. There he slept in the same room where Goodall had slept as a girl. He attended a nearby preparatory school. Grub was reunited with his mother on every holiday except for those he spent with his father.

The Kidnapping

The happiness of Goodall's new marriage was marred by a frightening event. On May 19, 1975, forty armed guerrilla soldiers from Zaire, the new nation across the lake from Tanzania, kidnapped four of the research center's student workers. The Zaireans were embroiled in political conflict with the Tanzanians. The guerrillas were not interested in the work being done at the Gombe research center. They believed the visiting white students would enhance their bargaining power and so they took the four students as hostages. The four, Emilie Bergman, Barbara Smuts, Kenneth Smith, and Jane Hunter, were seized late at night, tied up, and hustled into a stolen motorboat headed across Lake Tanganyika for Zaire. Hours later

Derek Bryceson, Goodall's second husband, addresses voters as he campaigns for reelection in a village at Masasi, Africa.

The Kidnapping

On May 19, 1975, Zairean guerrillas invaded the Gombe Stream Research Center and carried off four students. Writer Bettyann Kevles describes the event in Watching the Wild Apes.

"It was a Sunday evening, and the human population was asleep, except for the administrator, [Emilie] Bergman, who was up working late, her kerosene lamp burning in the window of her small hut on the slope. The first hint of trouble came at the beach where the Tanzanian staff lived. The boat that came out of the darkness surprised the park rangers when it spewed out a cargo of forty uniformed guerrillas who carried machine guns, rifles, and pistols, and spoke French and Lingala, a dialect popular in Zaire, across the lake. . . .

The raiders rushed onward to the light where Bergman was working. They ransacked her hut and grabbed her. Then they continued into another hut, where they surprised a young man. The sight of strangers speaking an unknown language startled him into shouts of 'Help!' Two women students rushed in, only to fall along with him and Bergman into the hands of the guerrillas, who bound them hand and foot and kidnapped them, taking along Gombe's only power boat as well. . . .

After a week, the soldiers rowed . . . one of the American women . . . the thirty-five miles back across Lake Tanganyika—a fifteen-hour trip—and deposited her on the lakeshore so that she could make her way into Kigoma. She brought with her the details of her capture and the demands of their captors. This ultimately led to difficult but successful negotiations. The other women were released first, and finally, at the end of August, the young man was freed too."

Grub's tutor ran to Goodall's house to report signs of a struggle—Emilie Bergman's typewriter had been found lying upside down on a path, and her hut had been ransacked. Emilie had been up late that night typing notes by lamplight. With a chill Goodall realized that if she had not turned out her own kerosene lamp early because of a sore eye, she too might have been kidnapped.

The Zairean guerrillas demanded the Tanzanian government give them $460,000 in cash and dozens of rifles. They also demanded the release of their

Kenneth Smith with his mother after his kidnapping and release by Zairean guerrillas. The incident would leave a permanent cloud over Goodall's Gombe Research Center.

comrades from jail. They released Bergman to explain their demands. She also carried the message that the remaining three students would be killed if the guerrillas did not get what they wanted.

During the government's negotiations with the kidnappers, everyone still at Gombe was asked to leave for their own safety. Goodall and her husband, along with several students, waited out this anxious episode at the Bryceson home in Dar es Salaam. Thanks to the pooled resources of the Tanzanian government, Stanford University, and the kidnapped students' parents, officials negotiated a deal with the guerrillas. Several weeks after their ordeal began, the remaining three students were at last safely released.

But the Gombe Stream Research Center would never be the same. According to Sy Montgomery: "From that time on, whites at Gombe were considered terrorist bait. Her African staff returned to the research station to take data on their own, but Jane was marooned at Dar es Salaam."[59] All of the center's precious research data was taken out of storage at Gombe and stored at the Bryceson home in Dar es Salaam for safekeeping. Until the threat of terrorism eventually faded after several years, Goodall visited her research center only in the company of armed guards.

Derek Bryceson, who spoke fluent Swahili as well as English and was well liked by Tanzanian officials and Goodall's African research staff, had proven invaluable during the crisis. According to Montgomery, Bryceson's "clout as director of Tanzania's national parks was crucial to resolving the kidnaping dilemma."[60] He also helped keep the research center going. According to Goodall in *My Life*, while the terrorist incident was being worked out, she and Bryceson visited the center twice to help and encourage the Tanzanian field staff who had been left behind to carry on the chimpanzee research:

> They did a wonderful job, but they needed a lot of guidance and help at first. But for Derek, the chimpanzee research might have ended then. . . . He helped me to build up a new research center, where almost all the observations were made by the Tanzanian field staff.[61]

The Chimpanzees Wage War

The kidnapping tested Goodall's faith in human nature. But for Goodall, an even greater blow came not as a result of human events, but in relation to new discoveries about her beloved chimps. As early as 1972 a group of six mature male chimpanzees, including Goliath, and three females had broken off from the original study group and moved south to set up a new community of their own. Researchers named the original group of chimpanzees the Kasakela group and the new offshoot the Kahama group. Increasingly, males from the old group had begun regular patrols to search out and kill the Kahama chimps.

Goodall had met the first reports of warfare among the chimpanzees with disbelief. According to Montgomery, she had seen the chimpanzees as mild mannered and friendly, even loving: "Watching these animals that men had seen as violent, maniacal, and murderous, Jane was most impressed by the chimps' gestures of gentle affection, their quest for comfort."[62]

John Mitani, a primatologist, speculates about why Goodall did not immediately grasp that the chimps were capable of brutality as well as gentleness. Perhaps she did not really want to see the truth, he suggests when quoted in *Walking with the Great Apes:*

> The picture painted of [apes] today is very different from what Goodall initially saw alone. . . . Goodall, like [primatologist Dian] Fossey, went into the field thinking these were cute, cuddly creatures. They were prone not to see things happening. . . . The single most important reason they didn't see these [negative] things . . . is the fact that they're tough animals to study, and these are rare events; but these women also had ingrained biases. And that isn't a criticism. . . . It points to the need for perseverance.[63]

However, when presented with clear evidence of the violence that could erupt between chimps, not even Goodall could deny that her initial assessment of their character had been flawed.

Attack on Goliath

One of the bloodiest incidents, witnessed by Emilie Bergman, occurred in 1975. Faben, a Kasakela chimp and one of old Flo's sons, led a group of five adult males and one adolescent male south. They reached a tree that they climbed and used as a lookout post, gazing toward Kahama territory. After about forty-five minutes Goliath, now old and almost toothless, came into view. Faben hooted and rushed toward the old chimpanzee, pushing him down. The rest of the chimps joined in, twisting Goliath's arms and legs, pounding him, biting him, and dragging him along the ground. The vicious attack lasted twenty minutes. Hooting triumphantly, throwing rocks and branches, and drumming on tree trunks, the Kasakela group left old Goliath to die. Emilie had no medical supplies with her, but the Gombe students and staff later returned to help him, only to discover that he had disappeared, never to be seen again.

Now only three Kahama males remained, and they too were soon exterminated. But before the last Kahama male met his fate, one of the three adult females, who had been named Madam Bee, was also attacked and killed. Goodall was shocked and sorrowful, for she had hoped that the females would be spared the senseless violence and perhaps be taken back into the Kasakela community. But after the last male was killed, no trace was found of the remaining two females, and so by late 1977 the entire Kahama community was wiped out in a space of about four years.

Cannibalism

As if this was not enough, the Gombe field staff radioed Goodall in Dar es Salaam with some unbelievable news in August 1975. One of the female chimpanzees, Passion, had teamed up with her adolescent daughter, Pom, and seized a three-week-old infant chimpanzee from its mother and killed it with a bite to the head. They then spent five hours eating the baby's body. Passion and Pom had committed cannibalism. It was not the first time cannibalism among chimps had been recorded. In 1970 a group of adult males had attacked a female from a neighboring community and seized her baby, killed it, and eaten part of the corpse. But the incident seemed unplanned, unlike the deliberate actions of Passion and Pom. In *Through a Window*, Goodall recalls:

> We were all dumfounded. . . . Passion's attack . . . seemed to have been directed to one end only—the capture of [the] baby. And the carcass was consumed in the way that normal prey is consumed, slowly and with relish, each mouthful of meat chewed up with a few green leaves.[64]

The Grisly Attacks Continue

The dead baby's mother, Gilka, gave birth to a new baby. Again Passion and Pom tried to kill it, but the first time this happened, Gilka screamed loudly and several males charged over and attacked Passion, who fled. However, Gilka's new baby ultimately met the same fate as the other. Pom attacked Gilka, who had crouched over her infant to protect it. While Pom hit Gilka, Passion seized the infant and sank her teeth into the front of its head, killing it instantly. Gilka tried to retrieve her baby, but Passion hurried off with the corpse, followed by Pom.

Passion, the chimpanzee whom Goodall witnessed killing the three-week-old baby of another chimpanzee. Passion repeated the incident several times. Goodall and her staff struggled with their impulse to interfere.

Pom (center) threatens Melissa (right), as the two fight over a salt lick at Goodall's camp. Gremlin (left), daughter of Melissa, offers support.

In November 1976 two Tanzanian staff members witnessed Passion and Pom attack the three-week-old daughter of a female named Melissa. During the attack Melissa's other daughter, a six-year-old named Gremlin, ran toward the researchers, stood upright and gazed into their eyes, then back at her struggling mother, as if she were asking the field staff for help. The assistants responded to her plea by throwing rocks at Passion and Pom, but the bloodthirsty chimps ignored the rocks. Melissa desperately clutched her baby to her chest as Passion held her down. Pom bit into the baby's head, killing it. Then Passion and Pom tugged until

Melissa was forced to let go of her dead infant's corpse, and Pom ran off with it.

The Fine Line Between Help and Interference

Goodall and her field staff debated what to do to stop the horrible incidents. They had, on occasion, provided help to the chimps during times of crisis. For example, in the late 1960s an epidemic of polio broke out in a nearby African village then spread to the chimpanzees. Goodall wired Nairobi for help, and a laboratory there

Seeking Nature's Healing

After only a few years of marriage, Jane Goodall's second husband, Derek Bryceson, died of cancer. Goodall recalls in Through a Window *that Gombe's natural setting provided a source of healing for her grief.*

"It was to Gombe that I went, seeking solace, after Derek lost his heroic battle with cancer. He died in Germany, where, for a while, we had hope for a miracle—a hope that we clutched at, desperately, as do thousands of others in similar circumstances. When hope was ended, I knew that bitterness and despair that comes to all of us when we lose one whom we have loved. I spent a little time with my family in England. Then back to Dar [es Salaam], with all its sad associations: gazing each day at the Indian Ocean where Derek, despite his crippled legs, had found freedom swimming among his beloved coral reefs. It was a real relief to leave the house and bury myself, for a while, in Gombe. For there I could hide my hurt among the ancient trees, find new strength for living in the forests that, surely, have changed little since Christ walked the hills of Jerusalem.

It was during that time, when I spent hours in the field with little thought of collecting data, that I came closer to the chimpanzees than ever before. For I was with them not to observe, to learn, but simply because I needed their company, undemanding and free of pity. And, as my spirit gradually healed, so I became increasingly aware of a new intuitive empathy with the chimpanzees, with these closest living relatives of ours. Ever since, I have felt more in tune with the natural world, the endless cycles of nature, the interdependence of all living things in the forest."

agreed to donate oral polio vaccine for Goodall, van Lawick, the staff, and the chimpanzees. The staff gave the chimps the vaccine by putting it into their bananas.

Goodall had helped ease chimpanzees' suffering on other occasions as well. She had given Gilka medication to control a fungal growth on her face. When Flo was dying of old age, she had given her eggs to make her last days happier ones. If chimps became ill, she gave them antibiotics. Many critics chastise Goodall for acting instead of standing by and merely watching events take their course. Goodall believed that humans had already interfered negatively in the lives of many animals and that a small amount of positive interference only evened the score.

Goodall and her staff discussed ways to stop the cannibalism of Passion and Pom. They considered catching Passion, tranquilizing her, and operating on her arm to disable it. But Goodall could not permit the permanent crippling of any chimpanzee. The operation would have to be reversible. No one could figure out how it could be accomplished. In four years a total of six more infants vanished, probably caught and eaten by Passion and Pom. But after first Passion and then Pom became pregnant themselves, the killings finally stopped.

"A Dark Side"

Both the brutal territorial raids and the infant killings deeply disillusioned Goodall. She writes:

> The intercommunity violence and the cannibalism that took place at Gombe . . . changed forever my view of chimpanzee nature. For so many years I had believed that chimpanzees, while showing uncanny similarities to humans in many ways were, by and large, rather "nicer" than us. Suddenly I found that under certain circumstances they could be just as brutal, that they also had a dark side to their nature. And it hurt. . . .

> Gradually, however, I learned to accept the new picture. For although the basic aggressive patterns of the chimpanzees are remarkably similar to some of our own, their comprehension of the suffering they inflict on their victims is very different from ours. Chimpanzees, it is true, are able to empathize, to understand at least to some extent the wants and needs of their companions. But only humans, I believe, are capable of *deliberate* cruelty—acting with the intention of causing pain and suffering.[65]

Goodall seems to be saying that although chimpanzees may have a dim idea of the suffering they inflict through violent behavior, they do not deliberately set out to hurt others the way humans may plot and plan to do so out of sheer meanness or desire for revenge. Humans, according to Goodall, are not only more sophisticated in their cruelty, but they also have a moral awareness of the rightness or wrongness of their actions that chimpanzees do not seem to have.

Although the worst finally seemed to have passed, Goodall was forced to undergo one more deeply painful event, this one occurring as the new decade began. In 1980, after they had been married only five years, her husband was stricken with cancer. By the time doctors realized Bryceson had cancer, it was already too late for treatment. But the Brycesons, desperate to find a cure, flew to Germany and Derek checked into an alternative medical clinic. Goodall stayed in a nearby lodging house while Bryceson received treatment. A few months later, in October 1980, he died. Goodall was heartbroken. Decades later she still wears the gold wedding band he gave her.

In the years since her arrival at Gombe, Jane Goodall had seen the best and the worst in both the apes and the humans she interacted with. She had endured much.

8 Crusading for Conservation

In recent years Jane Goodall has finally won the respect of the majority of her colleagues, especially after publishing a long, scholarly book detailing her scientific findings at Gombe called *The Chimpanzees of Gombe: Patterns of Behavior.* Finishing this challenging publication in 1986 left her with energy to spare. She channeled this energy into speaking out worldwide for the protection of chimpanzees, whose welfare had become endangered by illegal hunting, or poaching, and the destruction of their natural environment. Ironically, the more time Goodall devoted to saving the chimpanzees, the less time she had to spend observing them in the wilds of Gombe.

The Big Book

Goodall's 1986 book was different from her previous publications. She had written scholarly papers for her colleagues that had appeared in respected journals. And she had published popular books read by the public, such as *In the Shadow of Man,* that contained stories about Flo, David Greybeard, and the rest, as well as reflections on events in her own life, such as her first meeting with Louis Leakey or how

she and Hugo van Lawick raised their son at Gombe. This new book was different.

Goodall called it the Big Book, and the description fit. Its size and scope made an impression on her colleagues. According to writer Virginia Morell:

In a 1991 publicity photo, Goodall shows a poster advertising her campaign to save the chimpanzee.

Most of the remaining critics were silenced in 1986 by Goodall's book *The Chimpanzees of Gombe*. A [collection] of 25 years of research, filled with charts and graphs, the book demonstrated that she, too, could make "objective" generalizations about chimpanzees. But the essence of her work remained the perception of the individual personalities within the primate group.[66]

Goodall's facts, charts, and graphs satisfied the scientists in her field whose own methods relied on careful documentation. Her book's message remained the same as in all her works: that identifying with individual animals and trying to understand what they might be thinking and feeling is the basis for good ethology. She had managed to impress her critics without changing her theories to suit them.

Goodall Hesitates to Get Involved

Now that the Big Book was behind her, Goodall had energy for other matters. Many of her fellow primatologists, ethologists who studied apes, some of them former students, had grown increasingly frustrated with her seeming lack of interest in the issue of conservation. It was not that she failed to understand that chimpanzees were endangered by human activity to the point where they might become extinct. And she was painfully aware that chimps in captivity—in zoos, circuses, medical laboratories, and on movie sets—were often treated poorly or even cruelly. She had known these things for years. And yet she had never spoken out about protecting the chimpanzees. Her friends were frustrated with her silence.

Instead, before 1986 Goodall seemed content to concern herself with the relatively small group of chimpanzees she had become acquainted with at Gombe. She agonized over their welfare but did not use her famous name and scientific reputation to advance the cause of chimpanzee conservation. Perhaps her proper British upbringing kept her from speaking out; perhaps she sensed that becoming an activist would drain much of her energy, for when she threw herself into anything she cared about, she did so wholeheartedly.

Already, Goodall had done much for the chimpanzees at Gombe. In fact, if she had never gone to Gombe in 1960, there might have been no chimpanzees left there by 1986. She had arrived at Gombe at precisely the time when the local residents were trying to get the reserved status of Gombe changed. They wanted to regain the right to live by the lakeshores reserved for chimps, to move back in and develop the land, destroying the chimps' habitat in the process. Goodall's early findings about the chimps' tool use and meat eating, and the subsequent establishment of the Gombe Stream Research Center, ensured that Gombe would remain a safe place for the chimpanzees living there.

Frustrated Colleagues

But what about threatened chimpanzees living outside the Gombe center? While Goodall had briefly mentioned dangers facing chimpanzees, such as poaching, in her earlier books, she otherwise seemed to ignore the conservation issue. Geza

A Wild Chimp's Life Runs Cheap

Christophe Boesch and Hedwige Boesch-Achermann, two researchers who studied chimpanzees in the forests of Africa's Ivory Coast, conclude their Natural History *magazine article with a warning of how modern society threatens these animals.*

"Africa's tropical rain forests, and their inhabitants, are threatened with extinction by extensive logging, largely to provide the Western world with tropical timber and such products as coffee, cocoa, and rubber. . . . The climate has changed dramatically. . . . Rainfall has diminished. . . .

In addition, the chimpanzee, biologically very close to humans, is in demand for research on AIDS and hepatitis vaccines. Captive-bred chimps are available, but they cost about twenty times more than wild-caught animals. Chimps taken from the wild for these purposes are generally young, their mothers having been shot during capture. For every chimp arriving at its sad destination, nine others may well have died in the forest or on the way. Such priorities—cheap coffee and cocoa and chimpanzees—do not do the economies of Third World countries any good in the long run, and they bring suffering and death to innocent victims in the forest."

A mother and baby chimpanzee in the wild. Goodall campaigned against the practice of capturing baby chimps for research and zoos.

Teleki, a former student who had set up a national park in Sierra Leone, in West Africa, to protect chimps from being hunted for meat or captured and sent to medical research laboratories, remembers his frustration with Goodall's inaction:

The fact that she would not get involved really disappointed me. . . . I thought it was her responsibility, given her visibility. But she was very oriented toward individuals and very narrow about understanding general chimpanzee problems. She knew everything about Gombe and nothing about chimps anywhere else.[67]

Goodall had founded the Jane Goodall Institute for Wildlife Research, Education and Conservation in 1977, but the organization had done little more than publish a newsletter and make her books available to members. However, a weekend in Chicago in 1986 changed the casual focus of that organization and gave birth to a new one dedicated to helping the world's chimpanzees. Goodall was inspired by a November 1986 symposium called "Understanding Chimpanzees," organized by the Chicago Academy of Sciences. She and her fellow primatologists met to share new findings about the chimpanzees they studied. Instead, all they could talk about was whether or not there would be any chimpanzees left to study. Suddenly the realization of the danger facing the animals she had devoted her life to studying hit Goodall full force.

That very weekend she organized the Committee for the Conservation and Care of Chimpanzees (CCCC). This group concentrated on proving that chimps were in danger by collecting and documenting scientific details about their condition.

The group argued to lawmakers in Washington, D.C., that the apes should be listed as an endangered, rather than threatened, species. This new status would give them more international protection. The CCCC also lobbied to try to ensure that chimpanzees held in zoos or laboratories would have their physical and psychological needs met, such as enough light and room to move around and enough mental stimulation.

Speaking Out

After that November weekend Goodall was off and running. She spent most of the next two years, from 1986 to 1988, lobbying in Washington to reclassify chimpanzees as endangered. She appeared on countless television programs, such as *Donahue*, *20/20*, *Nightline*, and *Good Morning America*, to tell the public about the plight of captive and wild chimpanzees. She wrote articles on the subject for the *New York Times* and other major newspapers and magazines.

In Sy Montgomery's *Walking with the Great Apes*, Goodall considered the question of why she took so long to become active in the cause of chimpanzee conservation. She felt that she needed the extra respect that publishing *The Chimpanzees of Gombe* gave her before she could become a truly believable speaker for chimpanzee conservation: "Publishing [the book] gave me the credibility that maybe I would have lacked in scientific circles. I think in fact that destiny determined the exact right moment to launch myself into [the cause]. I could not have done the book *and* this."[68]

Goodall speaks at the National Press Club as part of her campaign to protect the wild chimpanzees and other primates. A powerful and moving speaker, Goodall has been able to motivate people to donate money for her project.

Becoming an activist cost Jane Goodall much. She had to give up time studying the chimpanzees at Gombe, work she loved, in order to commit to a heavy schedule of speaking engagements that publicized the plight of all chimpanzees. During the late 1980s and early 1990s, she spent about four months of each year at Gombe, four months writing at her home in Dar es Salaam, and four months raising money to support her Gombe research. Each spring she threw herself into a busy lecture tour in the United States, speaking to college students and other groups. The travel pace was hectic. Goodall rarely spent more than a few weeks in one place. Assistants from the Jane Goodall Institute took turns traveling with her on the lecture circuit. When he could, her son, now an adult, accompanied her.

Of her hectic schedule, Goodall writes, "I race from place to place, with never enough time anywhere." [69] But she always makes time to return to Gombe. The trouble of working a Gombe visit into her complex schedule is well worth it after the breakneck pace of the rest of her year:

All my problems fade away when I follow the chimps deep into the forest and sit with them. The birds sing. The wind whispers in the leaves. Little lizards move up and down the old trunks of trees. That, for me, is like a visit to heaven. . . .

I especially love being in the forests in the wet season. . . . In the dry season there always seem to be visitors around. But in the rainy months I am usually at Gombe by myself. And that, for me, is best.[70]

A Powerful Speaker

Goodall proved to be a powerful speaker. She radiates a quiet self-confidence from her slender and graceful frame, and her British-accented voice is gentle and melodious. Instead of bombarding her listeners with harsh facts and statistics about the harm being done to chimps, she shares stories, helping people get to know some of the chimpanzees they are being asked to help. In using her gift for storytelling to appeal to the emotions of her listeners, she has gained much support for her cause. According to Montgomery, "People listen to her because she is talking about individuals: chimps with histories and motives, who have fantasies and dreams, who mourn their dead and enjoy a good joke."[71]

The Story of Old Man

In her speeches Goodall always uses one particular story that she feels has special meaning. It is the story of a chimpanzee named Old Man who was rescued from captivity and placed with three female chimps on an island preserve in Florida. A young man named Marc was employed to feed the chimps but was warned not to get too close to them. Marc took the risk of trying to become friendly with Old Man.

He got closer to him every day until at last Old Man would accept a banana from his hand. The chimpanzee eventually allowed Marc to pet him and to play with him, but the three females were still afraid of Marc.

One day Marc slipped and fell, scaring the baby of one of the female chimps. The females rushed at Marc, defending the baby, who they thought was in trouble. One of them bit the young man's neck, and the others quickly surrounded him, biting him in the wrist and leg. Marc was sure he would be killed when Old Man rushed up to the female chimps and, one at a time, pulled them off Marc. Then Old Man stood guard, keeping the female chimpanzees away while Marc dragged himself to his boat and escaped. Marc was convinced that Old Man had deliberately saved his life.

Goodall always ends this story with a question:

> If a chimpanzee—one, moreover, who had been abused by humans—can reach out across the species barrier to help a human friend in need, then surely we, with our deeper capacity for compassion and understanding, can reach out to help the chimpanzees who need us, so desperately, today. Can't we?[72]

Another story Goodall has recounted in *My Life with the Chimpanzees* reflects the guilt she feels over her hesitation to get involved with helping the world's chimpanzee population sooner. It also speaks of her admiration for people who are willing to take a stand when they encounter actions they believe to be wrong. She relates how, as a young girl, she came upon some older boys torturing some crabs on the beach. When she demanded that they stop, the boys only laughed. She felt powerless to do anything more to save the poor creatures and wrote that she remembers with shame her failure to this day.

By contrast, Goodall wrote, when her son was five he noticed another boy in his preschool tormenting a caged rabbit by spraying it with water from a hose. When the boy refused to stop, Goodall's son picked a fight with him, even though the other boy was older and bigger. The teacher punished her son for fighting, but Goodall felt he had won a victory—his courage had saved the rabbit from further torment. She is proud of her son for acting on his beliefs, when she herself at his age had been too frightened to do the same.

No Wild-Eyed Activist

It would seem that the remainder of Jane Goodall's life will be devoted to public action to further her beliefs that chimpanzees should be safe and free from mistreatment. Most people probably would admire her resolve, even those who do not agree with her views. She does not alienate her listeners with wild-eyed pronouncements, and she makes clear in her speeches that she recognizes the positions of those taking opposing viewpoints. For example, she understands the need to use chimpanzees, who are the animals closest to humans in their biological makeup, for medical experiments, such as for AIDS and cancer research.

Jane Goodall's simple and direct style also has appeal for her younger audience. In 1988 she published a book for young readers titled *My Life with the Chimpanzees*. According to reviewer Kimberly Olson

Fakih, Goodall has found a wide and enthusiastic audience among children: "Known for her writings and *National Geographic* television programs, Jane Goodall is welcome in every classroom. Schoolchildren call her the Chimp Lady and ask her repeatedly if she really has eaten termites and other chimp foods. [She has.]"[73]

Most of the book tells of amusing or hair-raising incidents in her early life among the chimps at Gombe. In the last part of the book, Jane Goodall reflects on her life's choices and whether she is happy with what she has done:

> Even if the research had all the money needed, I would probably still go around and give talks, because I want to share what I know with as many people as possible. I have been very lucky in my life. I have known the excitement of watching wild, free animals. Thousands of people can never know that joy. But at least I can tell them about it.[74]

The last chapter speaks directly to the readers, suggesting ways in which they too can make a difference in the world when they grow up. She does not push for all children to become ethologists. No matter what their interests, she wants them to be aware that nonhuman animals have their own emotions, needs, and motives—that they, too, like children, have their own unique voices.

Through a Window

Goodall's next book after her autobiography for children was the 1990 *Through a Window*. While *In the Shadow of Man* cov-

Goodall speaks to street children in Tanzania. Although she spent more time on fund-raising, she continued to work with chimps, writing a second book, Through a Window.

ered Goodall's first several years at Gombe, *Through a Window* brought the thirty-year story up to the present. Some of the behavior that Goodall was only just beginning to learn about, such as chimpanzee mating practices, was covered in more depth. For example, when a female bears a child, she is not ready to mate again for several years, until the child is older. When she is ready to mate, the skin around her sex organs swells and becomes pink, a signal to all interested males nearby. Males usually quarrel and compete over who will mate with which eligible female, but at times one male can convince a female in heat to go off alone

with him by waving sticks and branches and motioning to her. If the female consents to follow him, the pair is said to be having a *consortship.* This consortship allows one male to have more of a chance to father a child, since while he is alone with the female of his choice no other males will intrude on them.

In *Through a Window* Goodall also discusses individual chimpanzee life stories, such as Melissa's, Figan's, and Gilka's, in more detail. Melissa, a social youngster, became a high-ranking female and gave birth to twin sons. She also lost one or two infants to Passion and Pom's cannibalism. Figan, Flo's second son, triumphed over

Overcoming Biology by Choice

In Through a Window *Goodall discusses the human capacity for evil and the corresponding capacity for overcoming it.*

"We are, indeed, a complex and endlessly fascinating species. We carry in our genes, handed down from our distant past, deep-rooted aggressive tendencies. Our patterns of aggression are little changed from those that we see in chimpanzees. But while chimpanzees have, to some extent, an awareness of the pain which they may inflict on their victims, only we, I believe, are capable of real cruelty—the deliberate infliction of physical or mental pain on living creatures despite, or even because of, our precise understanding of the suffering involved. Only we are capable of torture. Only we, surely, are capable of evil.

But let us not forget that human love and compassion are equally deeply rooted in our primate heritage, and in this sphere too our sensibilities are of a higher order of magnitude than those of chimpanzees. Human love at its best, the ecstasy deriving from the perfect union of mind and body, leads to heights of passion, tenderness and understanding that chimpanzees cannot experience. . . .

Thus, although our 'bad' is worse, immeasurably worse, than the worst conceivable actions of our closest living relatives [chimpanzees], let us take comfort in the knowledge that our 'good' can be incomparably better. Moreover we have developed a sophisticated mechanism—the brain—which enables us, if we will, to control our inherited aggressive hateful tendencies. Sadly, our success in this regard is poor. Nevertheless, we should remember that we alone among the life forms of this planet are able to overcome, by conscious choice, the dictates of our biological natures. At least, this is what I believe."

insecurity through his intelligence and determination to become the alpha, or top-ranking, male for several years. Gilka, a playful youngster, suffered a fungus infection that, when unchecked by medication, deformed her face. She also lost two infants to Passion's cannibalism. She maintained a strong bond with a brother, Evered, who was her companion in her final years.

Goodall also devotes chapters to various aspects of chimpanzee life, such as their interactions with baboons nearby, their wars over territory, mother-daughter and mother-son relationships, power seeking, love, and sex. Final chapters discuss humankind's failure to protect its closest relative, and the book's appendixes discuss chimpanzee exploitation and conservation.

Jane Goodall is arguably one of the Western world's best-known living scientists. Her Ridgefield, Connecticut, based Jane Goodall Institute now has branches in the United Kingdom and Canada. The institute has launched a research program, ChimpanZoo, to study zoo chimpanzees using the same methods used to observe wild chimps at Gombe and comparing the results.

In the thirty years since she first arrived at Gombe, Jane Goodall has grown and her public has grown with her. She has gained public respect, not merely just public attention, for both herself and for the primates she studies. She is fond of saying jokingly that the questions she hears from journalists are smarter now; they used to ask her whether she expected to see Tarzan. If her public has become wiser, so indeed has Goodall herself. At the conclusion of *Through a Window* she writes:

> It is thirty years since I began to study chimpanzees. Thirty years during which there has been much change in the world, including the way in which we think about animals and the environment. My own personal journeys during this period, through the peaceful forests of Gombe and through the thorny jungles that have sprung up around the issues of animal welfare and conservation, have led me a very long way from the naive young English girl who, with her mother, stepped so eagerly from the boat onto the Gombe beach. Yet she is still there, still part of the more mature me, whispering excitedly in my ear whenever I see some new or fascinating piece of chimpanzee behavior.[75]

Goodall's ability to hold onto her youthful burning curiosity about the world—a world that humankind is only a small part of—has been of lasting benefit to humans in search of knowledge about their place in the scheme of life.

Goodall is perhaps the most well known living scientist. She is one of the few scientists who has succeeded in communicating the importance of her work in a way an average person can understand.

9 Jane Goodall's Influence

Ever since Jane Goodall climbed the Peak with her binoculars and notepad and her sympathetic, nonthreatening attitude toward the wild chimpanzees of Gombe, the science of ethology has never been the same. Once dominated by scientists who believed in keeping an emotional distance from the animals they manipulated and experimented on, the field is now populated by scientists inspired by Jane Goodall's example of empathy and respect for the individual animal.

Characteristics of Goodall's Research Style

One of the characteristics of Goodall's research methods is the slow and patient approach she uses in gathering data. In her early months at Gombe, she kept her distance on the Peak, making herself visible to the chimpanzees but allowing them to get used to her presence thoroughly before approaching closer. Other scientists following in Goodall's footsteps have adopted this method, often taking years before gaining close contact with the primates and other animals they study.

Observing each animal as an individual being, rather than as a featureless compo-

nent of a larger group, is another characteristic of Goodall's research style. She names each chimpanzee she studies, basing the name on a quality that makes that chimp unique. She follows the life history of each chimpanzee as far as possible from birth to death. Followers of Goodall believe that her focus on the lives of individual chimpanzees helps to shed light on how the larger group of primates develops and changes over time. Goodall's work points out how the actions of individual chimps can influence in what direction the chimpanzee society as a whole may go. As Eleanor McLaughlin puts it in an appendix to Goodall's *The Chimpanzee: The Living Link Between "Man" and "Beast"*: "In its practice, [Goodall's] work has shown that the deepest understanding is not gained by reducing things into separate, isolated, even abstract components, but by the drawing together of all elements into an active pattern of change and development."[76]

Ivory Coast Researchers Inspired by Goodall

In 1979 researchers Christophe Boesch and Hedwige Boesch-Achermann began a long-term study of the rain forest chim-

Goodall with a chimp at Gombe Stream Research Center. Goodall inspired other researchers to imitate her unique style and study chimps in other areas of Africa.

panzees of Africa's Republic of the Ivory Coast. Following Goodall's example, the researchers followed the chimpanzees at a distance rather than capturing them for study. Like Goodall's Gombe chimpanzees the Ivory Coast chimps were shy and skittish around intruders. But according to Boesch and Boesch-Achermann, "After five years of fieldwork, we were finally able to follow the chimpanzees at close range, and gradually, we gained insights into their way of hunting."[77]

The findings about cooperative hunting and tool use among the Ivory Coast chimpanzees built on Goodall's early and important observations of chimps' using twigs as tools and hunting and sharing meat. According to Boesch and Boesch-Achermann: "Many anthropologists still hold that hunting cooperatively and sharing food played a central role in the drama that enabled early hominids [ancestral humans], some 1.8 million years ago, to develop the social systems that are so typically human."[78] Thus the exciting discoveries Goodall made about hunting techniques and tool use are still being eagerly pursued by her colleagues in an effort to understand the links and differences between primates and humans.

Sy Montgomery and the Emus

Sy Montgomery, the writer of a book about Jane Goodall and two other primatologists called *Walking with the Great Apes*, discusses in her book's preface the great influence Jane Goodall had over her own research style. Montgomery was commissioned by the Chicago Zoological Society to study plants and their nitrogen cycles in Australia. On her own time she also began to study emus, the ancient, human-sized flightless birds that live there. Montgomery was already familiar with Goodall's work methods. She deliberately imitated these techniques when approaching the huge, strange birds. According to Montgomery:

I reminded myself that although I had no formal scientific training, neither did Jane when she began her study. I remembered how she acclimated the animals to her presence, and I did the same: each day I wore the same clothing . . . so they could easily recognize me. Like Jane, I approached the animals only to a point where they were clearly comfortable; I never wanted them to feel I was pursuing them. . . . I would enter their lives on their terms.[79]

Life on Their Terms

In Walking with the Great Apes, *scientist and journalist Sy Montgomery discusses the influence of Jane Goodall's style of research on her own scientific studies.*

"In a way our studies could not have been more different: she was studying chimpanzees, animals so closely related to man that blood transfusions between the two species are possible. I was studying beings more closely related to dinosaurs than to humans. She worked in a jungle, I in a scrub desert. She has continued her study for three decades; I knew I had to return to the States in six months. Nonetheless, I modeled my approach on hers. I remembered how she acclimated the animals to her presence, and I did the same: each day I wore the same clothing—jeans, the shirt I slept in, my father's billowing green army jacket, and a red kerchief, so they could easily recognize me. Like Jane, I approached the animals only to a point where they were clearly comfortable; I never wanted them to feel I was pursuing them. I did not want to steal from them, not even glimpses; I asked only that they show me what they chose to. I would enter their lives on their terms."

During the six months that Montgomery followed the emus and recorded their behavior, she developed an emotional attachment to them similar to Goodall's own affection and empathy for the Gombe chimpanzee. She writes:

> On my last day . . . I went out again to the emus. They seemed to be looking for me. I followed them all day, and toward evening they stopped to graze on some wild mustard. Then I thought: I wish I could tell you what you have given me. How could I express to creatures whose experience of the world was so different from mine what they had allowed me to feel?[80]

Montgomery calls the feeling the emus conjured in her love. The emotional connection between Montgomery and the emus mirrors Goodall's own personal and sympathetic relationship with the Gombe chimpanzees.

Conservation and Reserves

In addition to developing a new research style that was adopted by other primatologists and animal researchers, Jane Goodall is responsible for inspiring a heightened public awareness of anticruelty and conservation issues. Her official vehicle for conveying such messages to the public is the Jane Goodall Institute for Wildlife Research, Education and Conservation. Goodall heads the nonprofit organization dedicated to studying chimpanzees and conserving their habitat. The institute sponsors field research on wild chimpanzees, as well as funding studies of captive chimpanzees, comparing their behavior to that in the wild. The institute also funds conservation programs in Africa to protect chimpanzees from the consequences of the destruction of Africa's rain forests and from the local shooting and selling of chimpanzees for profit.

The Gombe Stream Research Center, where Goodall began her groundbreaking work, is still dedicated to the study of the Gombe chimpanzees. Currently there are about 150 chimpanzees living in three communities within the forested, mountainous reserve. A field study of the chimps in the Kasakela community has continued unbroken since Goodall began it in 1960. Researchers at Gombe are currently studying the behavior and ecology of chimpanzees, olive baboons, and red colobus monkeys, as well as researching the potential medicinal uses of forest plant life.

The Jane Goodall Institute spends about forty thousand dollars each year maintaining chimpanzee reserves in the Congo and in Kenya. Another reserve is currently under development in Burundi, near Tanzania, at Kibira National Park. At this reserve the Jane Goodall Institute is studying the ecology and behavior of the local chimp population. The institute is cooperating with Kibira residents to try to habituate a group of the chimpanzees to the presence of humans. This would allow the development of a tourist industry that would aid Kibira economically, while discouraging poaching and destructive logging practices that endanger the chimps.

Sanctuaries

Goodall's organization sponsors several sanctuaries in Africa for chimpanzees that

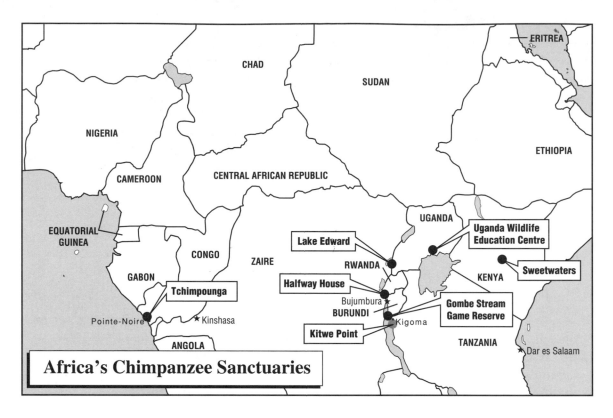

Africa's Chimpanzee Sanctuaries

have been illegally captured and abandoned or sold as pets. Many of these chimps were orphaned when their mothers were shot and killed for food. Orphaned chimpanzees are assigned a guardian, a person who contributes at least one hundred dollars each year for the rehabilitation and conservation of rescued chimpanzees in sanctuaries. Donations are applied to the cost of food, shelter, and medical supplies for sanctuary chimps.

The sanctuaries also provide employment opportunities to Africans, giving them alternatives to poaching and other illegal activities that endanger chimpanzees. In addition, the existence of sanctuaries provides African governments with a place to send illegally captured chimps, making officials more likely to enforce laws against this practice.

Sixteen zoos in the United States now participate in the institute's ChimpanZoo program, gathering and analyzing data on chimpanzee behavior in captivity. About 130 chimpanzees are involved in the program. ChimpanZoo's research results are presented each year at a week-long conference that is open to the public. Chimpan-Zoo's research findings, in addition to being published in scientific journals, are also made available to young people. The goals of the ChimpanZoo program, according to the Jane Goodall Institute, are to increase public awareness of chimpanzees and their behavior, to assist zoos in improving conditions for captive chimps, to exchange information on ways to improve conditions for captive chimps, and to compile information on chimpanzee behavior in a national database.

Goodall Receives Edinburgh Award

In 1991 Jane Goodall was awarded the Edinburgh Medal, which honors scientists who have made a contribution to the understanding and well-being of humanity. Eleanor McLaughlin praises her in the awards ceremony introduction, as reprinted in Goodall's The Chimpanzee.

"Without doubt Jane Goodall's work has been one of the great scientific projects of this century. It was commenced with no official scientific training or qualifications, and we should not hide from ourselves that that may well have been an advantage. In its practice, her work has shown that the deepest understanding is not gained by reducing things into separate, isolated, even abstract components, but by the drawing together of all elements into an active pattern of change and development.

Such a reaffirmation of a rich and productive scientific method is to her own great credit. In addition, the product of that method has revolutionised our understanding of humanity's place in nature and even of what society is, for the results have shown that, in contrast to the common view of humans being the very apex [summit] of creation, there are other tool-using, communicating, social primates, the chimpanzees, right alongside us.

This knowledge has been conveyed to us not only in scientific papers and monographs but in books for both children and adults which, whilst rigorously scientific, are also readily understandable. These publications and her work through the Jane Goodall Institute have been very influential in bringing about the improvement of conditions for primates in both captivity and the wild."

Goodall's work went beyond making scientific discoveries. She tried to get the public involved in preventing the destructive practice of obtaining wild chimps and the destruction of Africa's animal habitats.

Efforts to increase environmental awareness among young people led to the creation of Roots and Shoots, an international club for young people. It gets its name because Goodall considers children a fertile ground where seeds can grow, take root, and send out shoots that have the potential to change the world. The Roots and Shoots youth program promotes hands-on activities that lead to an understanding of environmental, animal, and community issues. Clubs are encouraged to teach such skills as community building, leadership, problem solving, investigation, and communication. Young people in the program learn how to observe and understand the world around them while becoming active in environmental and humanitarian issues.

The Founding Mother

Perhaps even more important than her establishment of the Jane Goodall Institute is Goodall's inspiring example to women primatologists who came after her. Virginia Morell cites the example of Melissa Remis, a Yale University doctoral candidate who studied lowland gorillas in central Africa. In the style of Jane Goodall, Remis allowed the gorillas to slowly become used to her so that she could study their normal behavior patterns. Before she achieved this goal, Remis endured four-hundred-pound screaming gorillas rushing at her. She crouched and clung to a tree trunk during these vocal assaults, calling up the memory of Jane Goodall and another primatologist, Dian Fossey.

Fossey, who studied mountain gorillas in Rwanda, Africa, until her death in 1985,

and Birute Galdikas, who began her studies of orangutans in Borneo, Indonesia, in 1971, also adopted Goodall's style of observing animals in the wild. Sy Montgomery describes this approach as giving up control of the situation to the ape, allowing the relationship between human researcher and animal subject to develop slowly: "Dian Fossey and Birute Galdikas modeled their approach on Jane Goodall's: they began their studies by [giving up] control. . . . This approach allows choice and the nurturing of a relationship on the other's terms."[81]

Dian Fossey

Goodall, Fossey, and Galdikas eventually came to be known as the *trimates*, a nickname ethologists made up for the three from the word *primate* and the Latin prefix meaning "three." Fossey began her gorilla research in 1967. As with Goodall, her primary sponsor was Louis Leakey. Leakey arranged for Fossey's first stop on her journey to be a visit to Goodall at Gombe. In her book *Gorillas in the Mist*, Fossey recalls:

> When all of the gear was finally assembled, Jane Goodall kindly invited me to visit the Gombe Stream Research Centre for two days to show me her methods of camp organization, data collecting, and, as well, to introduce me to her lovable chimpanzees. I fear that I was not an appreciative guest, for I was desperately keen to reach Kabara [Zaire] and the mountain gorillas.[82]

Fossey made many important discoveries about gorillas, but she often felt over-

Goodall greatly inspired Dian Fossey (pictured), who imitated her methods while she studied the mountain gorilla.

shadowed by Goodall. Sy Montgomery writes of Fossey's jealousy over the attention Goodall received:

> Neither Dian nor her gorillas seemed able to compete successfully with Jane and her chimps for the limelight. Dian made important discoveries about gorilla life. . . . But these discoveries were outshone by Jane's findings about chimpanzee hunting and tool use, cannibalism and warfare—behavioral aspects that made the chimps seem more like man.[83]

Birute Galdikas

Like Goodall and Fossey, Birute Galdikas began her work as an orangutan re-

searcher under the guidance of Louis Leakey. And, like the other two trimates, Galdikas's research methods are one part empathy, one part determination, and a large portion of patience. Galdikas is recognized as a leader in orangutan research, for she has recorded and reported much new information about the lives and behavior of these apes.

Thanks to the groundbreaking work of primatologists such as Goodall, Fossey, and Galdikas, more women have entered the field, and female contributions have become more respected. According to Morell, writing in 1991, "North American primatology, two decades ago a male preserve, is today more than 50% female." Their methods have become the standard: "Today, after many battles, the significance of the individual personality in primate groups is taken for granted, and the three women are seen as pathbreakers."[84]

Goodall, Fossey, and Galdikas did not listen to other scientists' warnings about becoming emotionally involved with their subjects. Instead, they opened themselves up to the unknown and forged relation- ships that allowed new scientific discover- ies to emerge. In so doing, they have for- ever changed humankind's understanding of its relationship to other animals.

Jane Goodall's legacy has extended be- yond the immediate environment of the Gombe Stream Research Center. Her style

A Biologist Praises Goodall

At the Third Edinburgh Medal Address, biologist Aubrey Manning gives Jane Goodall, the recipient of the 1991 Edinburgh Medal for humanitarian achievement in science, a vote of thanks. This excerpt was reprinted in Goodall's The Chimpanzee.

"I think that Jane Goodall's work has profound signifi- cance for us in a number of ways. I think the first way was for biologists as she really showed us that it was possible. Until news began to emerge of her results in Gombe, most of us would not have thought that it was feasible to gain such information from wild animals. As a result of her pioneering achievements an enormous number of studies have been carried out on many other primates, but she was the true leader.

To do such work required great physical courage. . . . Her work also has profound significance in another way: it has shown us that chimpanzees are magnificently themselves. I don't think, frankly, that we have much to learn in behavioural terms from chimpanzees. What we can learn from them is the much more profound lesson that they are themselves and we ought to give them the space to be themselves. For me this is really the most im- portant lesson of all.

As Jane has so eloquently told us, it will require a great deal of work and sacrifice from us if the chim- panzees are to survive, and survive in the way that they deserve. She has shown us what they require and, in do- ing so, has revealed some hints of how to restore that vi- tal balance between humanity and the other living things with which we share the planet. The lesson is important, obviously, for the chimpanzees who are greatly and im- mediately threatened but I think the point is also one for our own survival."

Indonesian president Suharto greets Goodall and Birute Galdikas, whose pioneering research on orangutans was heavily influenced by Goodall.

and methods have inspired additional research on the links between humans and apes; her institute's many programs have improved conditions for chimpanzees and added to public understanding of the interconnectedness between humans and chimpanzees; and her work in a formerly male-dominated field has been an inspiration to women primatologists who have come after her. Goodall's research still continues, providing a wealth of observation and analysis of the creatures that more closely resemble human beings than any other.

Notes

Chapter 1: The Young Naturalist

1. Jane Goodall, *My Life with the Chimpanzees.* New York: Pocket Books, 1988, p. 2.
2. Jane Goodall, *In the Shadow of Man.* Boston: Houghton Mifflin, 1971, p. 3.
3. Goodall, *My Life with the Chimpanzees*, p. 13.
4. Quoted in Ron Arias, "Jane Goodall," *People Weekly*, May 14, 1990, p. 98.
5. Goodall, *My Life with the Chimpanzees*, p. 13.
6. Goodall, *My Life with the Chimpanzees*, p. 22.
7. Goodall, *My Life with the Chimpanzees*, p. 26.
8. Goodall, *My Life with the Chimpanzees*, pp. 26–27.
9. Goodall, *My Life with the Chimpanzees*, p. 28.
10. Sy Montgomery, *Walking with the Great Apes.* Boston: Houghton Mifflin, 1991, p. 29.

Chapter 2: Into Africa

11. Goodall, *My Life with the Chimpanzees*, p. 34.
12. Goodall, *My Life with the Chimpanzees*, p. 35.
13. Montgomery, *Walking with the Great Apes*, p. 78.
14. Goodall, *My Life with the Chimpanzees*, p. 38.
15. Goodall, *In the Shadow of Man*, p. 6.
16. Goodall, *In the Shadow of Man*, pp. 8–9.
17. Goodall, *In the Shadow of Man*, p. 12.
18. Bettyann Kevles, *Watching the Wild Apes: The Primate Studies of Goodall, Fossey, and Galdikas.* New York: E. P. Dutton, 1976, p. 17.
19. Goodall, *In the Shadow of Man*, p. 16.

Chapter 3: The Work Begins

20. Montgomery, *Walking with the Great Apes*, p. 94.
21. Goodall, *In the Shadow of Man*, p. 17.
22. Goodall, *In the Shadow of Man*, p. 95.

23. Jane Goodall, *My Friends the Wild Chimpanzees.* Washington, DC: National Geographic Society, 1967, p. 32.
24. Goodall, *My Friends*, p. 32.
25. Virginia Morell, "Called 'Trimates,' Three Bold Women Shaped Their Field," *Science*, April 16, 1993, p. 421.
26. Quoted in Morell, "Called 'Trimates,'" pp. 421–22.

Chapter 4: Acceptance

27. Goodall, *In the Shadow of Man*, p. 4.
28. Goodall, *In the Shadow of Man*, p. 50.
29. Goodall, *In the Shadow of Man*, p. 49.
30. Joyce A. Senn, *Jane Goodall: Naturalist.* Woodbridge, CT: Blackbirch Publishers, 1993, p. 33.

Chapter 5: Establishing an Identity

31. Montgomery, *Walking with the Great Apes*, pp. 102–103.
32. Jane Goodall, *Through a Window: My Thirty Years with the Chimpanzees of Gombe.* Boston: Houghton Mifflin, 1990, p. 11.
33. Morell, "Called 'Trimates,'" p. 422.
34. Morell, "Called 'Trimates,'" p. 422.
35. Montgomery, *Walking with the Great Apes*, p. 102.
36. Goodall, *Through a Window*, p. 16.
37. Goodall, *Through a Window*, p. 17.
38. Morell, "Called 'Trimates,'" p. 422.
39. Quoted in Montgomery, *Walking with the Great Apes*, p. 105.
40. Quoted in Montgomery, *Walking with the Great Apes*, p. 106.
41. Goodall, *Through a Window*, p. 16.

Chapter 6: Gombe Blossoms

42. Goodall, *In the Shadow of Man*, p. 75.

43. Goodall, *In the Shadow of Man*, p. 75.

44. Montgomery, *Walking with the Great Apes*, p. 29.

45. Quoted in Arias, "Jane Goodall," p. 99.

46. Montgomery, *Walking with the Great Apes*, p. 40.

47. Goodall, *Through a Window*, p. 24.

48. Goodall, *Through a Window*, p. 24.

49. Kevles, *Watching the Wild Apes*, p. 49.

50. Goodall, *Through a Window*, p. 25.

51. Goodall, *In the Shadow of Man*, p. 114.

52. Goodall, *In the Shadow of Man*, p. 118.

53. Kevles, *Watching the Wild Apes*, p. 30.

54. Kevles, *Watching the Wild Apes*, pp. 49–50.

55. Montgomery, *Walking with the Great Apes*, p. 108.

56. Kevles, *Watching the Wild Apes*, p. 55.

Chapter 7: Tragedy in Paradise

57. Quoted in Arias, "Jane Goodall," p. 99.

58. Goodall, *My Life with the Chimpanzees*, p. 85.

59. Montgomery, *Walking with the Great Apes*, p. 122.

60. Montgomery, *Walking with the Great Apes*, p. 126.

61. Goodall, *My Life with the Chimpanzees*, pp. 89–90.

62. Montgomery, *Walking with the Great Apes*, p. 97.

63. Quoted in Montgomery, *Walking with the Great Apes*, p. 119.

64. Goodall, *Through a Window*, pp. 77–78.

65. Goodall, *Through a Window*, p. 108–109.

Chapter 8: Crusading for Conservation

66. Morell, "Called 'Trimates,' " p. 423.

67. Quoted in Montgomery, *Walking with the Great Apes*, p. 198.

68. Quoted in Montgomery, *Walking with the Great Apes*, p. 202.

69. Goodall, *My Life*, p. 104.

70. Goodall, *My Life*, p. 105.

71. Montgomery, *Walking with the Great Apes*, p. 206.

72. Goodall, *Through a Window*, p. 234.

73. Kimberly Olson Fakih, "Jane Goodall Eats Bugs—YUK!" *Publishers Weekly*, January 29, 1988, p. 396.

74. Goodall, *My Life with the Chimpanzees*, pp. 103–104.

75. Goodall, *Through a Window*, p. 235.

Chapter 9: Jane Goodall's Influence

76. Quoted in Jane Goodall, *The Chimpanzee: The Living Link Between "Man" and "Beast."* Edinburgh, Scotland: Edinburgh University Press, 1992, p. 47.

77. Christophe Boesch and Hedwige Boesch-Achermann, "Dim Forest, Bright Chimps," *Natural History*, September 1991, p. 53.

78. Boesch and Boesch-Achermann, "Dim Forest, Bright Chimps," p. 52.

79. Montgomery, *Walking with the Great Apes*, pp. xiv–xv.

80. Montgomery, *Walking with the Great Apes*, pp. xvii–xviii.

81. Montgomery, *Walking with the Great Apes*, p. xvi.

82. Dian Fossey, *Gorillas in the Mist.* Boston: Houghton Mifflin, 1983, p. 5.

83. Montgomery, *Walking with the Great Apes*, p. 149.

84. Morell, "Called 'Trimates,' " p. 420.

For Further Reading

Ron Arias, "Jane Goodall," *People Weekly*, May 14, 1990. A chatty article summarizing Jane Goodall's life and profiling her as a personality.

Jane Goodall, *My Friends the Wild Chimpanzees*. Washington, DC: National Geographic Society, 1967. An entertaining account of Jane Goodall and Hugo van Lawick's early years at Gombe.

———, *My Life with the Chimpanzees*. New York: Pocket Books, 1988. Goodall's autobiography written for children at the sixth- to seventh-grade reading level. Entertaining, filled with hair-raising stories of her early days at Gombe.

Bettyann Kevles, *Watching the Wild Apes: The Primate Studies of Goodall, Fossey, and Galdikas*. New York: E. P. Dutton, 1976. A study for young people of the three major figures in primatology. All three women worked with Louis Leakey, and Dian Fossey and Birute Galdikas were influenced by Jane Goodall's pioneering work.

Sy Montgomery, *Walking with the Great Apes*. Boston: Houghton Mifflin, 1991. A thoughtful, well-written study of the work of primatologists Jane Goodall, Birute Galdikas, and Dian Fossey.

Joyce A. Senn, *Jane Goodall: Naturalist*. Woodbridge, CT: Blackbirch Publishers, 1993. An easy-to-read, enjoyable discussion of Goodall's life and work.

Works Consulted

Christophe Boesch and Hedwige Boesch-Achermann, "Dim Forest, Bright Chimps," *Natural History*, September 1991. A summary of the authors' work with chimpanzees, which was influenced by the work of Jane Goodall.

Kimberly Olson Fakih, "Jane Goodall Eats Bugs—YUK!" *Publishers Weekly*, January 29, 1988. Jane Goodall's book for young people, *My Life with the Chimpanzees*, is reviewed, and her message to young people is explored.

Dian Fossey, *Gorillas in the Mist*. Boston: Houghton Mifflin, 1983. Dian Fossey's own account of her study of the mountain gorilla. Her life inspired a major motion picture of the same title.

Jane Goodall, *The Chimpanzees of Gombe: Patterns of Behavior*. Cambridge, MA: Harvard University Press, 1986. Jane Goodall's Big Book, the definitive collection of her thirty years of study at Gombe. Contains numerous illustrations and a chimpanzee who's who section.

———, *The Chimpanzee: The Living Link Between "Man" and "Beast."* Edinburgh, Scotland: Edinburgh University Press, 1992. In an illustrated lecture for the Third Edinburgh Medal Address, Goodall gives an overview of her pioneering work.

———, *In the Shadow of Man*. Boston: Houghton Mifflin, 1971. A detailed, entertaining account of Jane Goodall's first ten years at Gombe.

———, *Through a Window: My Thirty Years with the Chimpanzees of Gombe*. Boston: Houghton Mifflin, 1990. Jane Goodall's sensitively written reflections on her thirty years with the Gombe chimpanzees, highlighting the cannibalism and warfare as well as the life histories of selected chimps. Also contains appendixes on conservation.

Virginia Morell, "Called 'Trimates,' Three Bold Women Shaped Their Field," *Science*, April 16, 1993. The work of Goodall, Fossey, and Galdikas is discussed from the perspective of their gender in a formerly male-dominated field. Women scientists in other fields of study are highlighted in boxes.

Index

Africa, chimpanzee
    sanctuaries in, 98
*Annals of the New York
    Academy of Science*, 56

Bergman, Emilie, 74, 75,
    79
  kidnapping of, 76
Bryceson, Derek, 78
  death of, 82, 83
  marriage to Goodall, 75
Burroughs, Edgar Rice, 15

Cambridge University, 52,
    58
Carpenter, Clarence Ray,
    34
Chicago Academy of
    Sciences, 87
Chicago Zoological
    Society, 96
chimpanzees
  aggressive behavior of,
    48–49, 78–81
  cannibalism among,
    80–81
  communication by, 61
  consortship of, 91
  David Greybeard, 40, 49,
    50, 59
  Evered, 92
  Faben, 79
  Fifi, 47, 58, 72
  Figan, 47, 72
  Flint, 63, 72
  Flo, 63–65, 79
  Gilka, 80, 91
  Goliath, 40, 48, 49, 59,
    71, 79

  Goodall's close contact
    with, 72
Goodall's first observa-
    tions of, 36–38
  Gremlin, 80
  groups of, at Gombe, 79
  infant behavior, 40
  Ivory Coast, 95
  maternal behavior of,
    63–65
  mating practices of, 91
  Melissa, 80, 91
  Mike, 50, 69–70
  Old Man, 89
  Olly, 40
  Passion, 80
  Pom, 80
  rain dance of, 47
  sanctuaries for, 97–98
  sleeping habits of, 40
  threats to survival of, 86
  tool-making behavior of,
    41–42
  William, 59
*Chimpanzees of Gombe:
    Patterns of Behavior, The*
    (Goodall), 84, 85, 87
ChimpanZoo, 93, 98
Committee for the Con-
    servation and Care of
    Chimpanzees (CCCC),
    87
Congo, riots in, 31–32
Coryndon Memorial
    Museum of Natural
    History, 23

Dar es Salaam, Tanzania,
    75, 76

emus, 96
ethology, 54

Fossey, Dian, 100–101
Galdikas, Birute, 100, 101
Gombe Stream Game
    Reserve, 27
  chimpanzees of, 41
  Goodall's first trip to,
    31–32
  importance of Goodall's
    work at, 85
  map of, 29
  research center at
    current studies at, 97
    growth of, 67–68
    kidnapping of students
      from, 76–78
    was pawn in interstate
      conflict, 74
  wildlife of, 45
Goodall, Jane
  arrival at Gombe Stream
    Game Reserve, 32–33
  arrival in Kenya, 22
  at Olduvai Gorge dig, 26
  awards received by
    Edinburgh Medal, 99
    Franklin Burr Award,
      58
  becomes conservation
    advocate, 87–88
  Bryceson's death and, 82
  Cambridge University
    career of, 53–54
    earns doctorate, 58
  childhood of, 11
  criticism of, 57–58, 66,
    71, 73
  discovers chimps' tool-
    making behavior,
    40–41

  disillusionment about
    chimps, 83
  divorce from van Lawick,

74–75
early days at Gombe, 32–38
early schooling of, 15, 17–18
first job of, 18
first trip to Africa, 19–20
illness of, 38
job at Oxford University, 18–19
life during World War II, 13–15
marriage
    to Bryceson, 75
    to van Lawick, 62–63
meeting with Louis Leakey, 23–24
on hyena behavior, 64
on Lolui Island, 30–31
research style of, 94
return to England, 52
study of chimps in London, 28
views on ethology, 55
work as film librarian for Granada Television, 28
Goodall, Vanne. *See* Joseph, Margaret Myfanwe
Gorillas in the Mist (Fossey), 100
Granada Television, 28

Hinde, Robert, 58
Homo habilis, 25
Hunter, Jane, kidnapping of, 76
hyenas, 64

imprinting, 54

Jane Goodall Institute for Wildlife Research, Education, and Conservation, 87, 93, 97

Jolly, Alison, 43
Joseph, Margaret Myfanwe (mother), 12, 15
    as Jane's companion at Gombe, 29
    operates medical clinic at Gombe, 44–45
    returns to England, 47
Jungle Book, The (Kipling), 15

Kakombe Stream Valley, 38
Kibira National Park (Burundi), 97
Kigoma, Tanzania, 31
Kipling, Rudyard, 15

Leakey, Louis, 51, 59
    criticism of Goodall, 73
    early support of Goodall, 29–31
    first meeting with Goodall, 23–25
    Goodall's education and, 52
    reaction to tool-making discovery, 42–44
    relationship with Goodall, 37–38
    sponsorship
        of Fossey, 100
        of Galdikas, 101
    views on women, 26
Leakey, Mary, 59
Lofting, Hugh, 15
Lolui Island (Lake Victoria), 30
Lorenz, Konrad, 54

Manning, Aubrey, 102
Mbrisho (villager), 44
McLaughlin, Eleanor, 99
Mitani, John, 79
Morris-Goodall, Mortimer

Herbert (father), 12

National Geographic, 51, 57, 62
National Geographic Society, 51, 59, 66
    awards Goodall Franklin Burr Award, 58
    funding of Goodall's research by, 44, 68
Nyerere, Julius, 75

Olduvai Gorge, 24, 26
On Safari (TV series), 59

the Peak, 38, 60
Remis, Melissa, 100
Reveille (British newspaper), 51
Reynolds, Vernon, 34
Roots and Shoots youth program, 100

Smith, Kenneth, kidnapping of, 76
Smuts, Barbara, kidnapping of, 76
Stanford University, 78
Story of Dr. Dolittle, The (Lofting), influence on Goodall, 15

Teleki, Geza, 87

van Lawick
    Hugh, 59
    Hugo Eric Louis (Grub), 65–66

Wilkie, Leighton, 27

Zinjanthropus, 25

Credits

Photos

Cover photo: H. van Lawick © National Geographic Society Image Collection

AP/Wide World Photos, 50, 57, 60, 84, 95

© Archive Photos, 20, 66, 74, 75,

© Archive Photos/Lee, 93

© Archive Photos/Ralph Merlino, 99

Derek Bryceson © National Geographic Society Image Collection, 80, 81

The Courrier Journal, 101

© Nigel J. Dennis/Photo Researchers, Inc., 31, 40, 46

Jane Goodall © National Geographic Society Image Collection, 43

Hulton Deutsch, 19, 28, 62

© George Hulton/Photo Researchers, Inc., 10

© Tom McHugh/Photo Researchers, Inc., 86

National Archives, 14

Michael K. Nichols © National Geographic Society Image Collection, 91

Reuters/Bettmann, 103

H. van Lawick © National Geographic Society Image Collection, 36, 37, 45, 48, 63, 69, 71

UPI/Bettmann, 9, 23, 25, 26, 53, 54, 76, 78, 88

Text

Quotations from *My Life with the Chimpanzees* by Jane Goodall, © 1988 by Jane Goodall (New York: Pocket Books), are reprinted by permission of Byron Preiss Visual Publications and General Licensing Co., on behalf of the author.

About the Author

Paula Bryant Pratt graduated from Reed College and completed her graduate study at San Diego State University. She has been an in-house editor at Harcourt Brace and Company and a freelance author and editor. She has also taught community college English composition and creative writing. Currently she is community editor for a small daily newspaper. She is the author of Lucent Books' *The Importance of Martha Graham, Maps: Plotting Places on the Globe, Architecture,* and *The End of Apartheid in South Africa.* Paula and her husband, Michael, have a four-year-old daughter, Cerise Olivia.